Israel for Families
An Adventure in 12 Days

*An Innovative Guide to Exploring Israel
and Enriching Your Experience*

From the Team at RealFamilyTrips.com

Dedicated to our dear children, Noah, Julia, Anna, Sophia, Avery and Vera. You move, inspire, and motivate us; you make this world a better place by your presence. Sharing life's journey with each of you makes every day a blessing.

All Our Love,
Mommy and Daddy

Table of Contents

Introduction

Israel is many things to many people: a land of rich history and a melting pot of culture, a beautiful and vibrant land sprung up from the desert, a place that has known its share of turmoil, yet persists as a location filled with beauty, warm and vibrant citizens, as well as hope and inspiration. Well known for being among the holiest places in the world for Jews, Christians, and Muslims, the land of Israel has been inhabited and cherished for thousands of years. Modern Israel exists as a wonderful marriage of modernity and antiquity, at once preserved in time and leading the push into the modern era.

Modern Israel, founded in 1948, has grown quickly into a world power and a contemporary nation with a robust infrastructure. This is juxtaposed against relics from times past in a truly unique way. Hebrew and Arabic serve dually as official languages. A rich population of nationalities from around the world flourishes.

The geography of Israel is as diverse as its people, with the majestic hilly and mountainous regions of Golan, Carmel and Galilee, the sprawling Negev Desert, all mere miles away from the glittering Mediterranean coast. Straddling lines of temperate and tropical zones, Israel stays warm throughout the year, though in the summer months certain areas can actually get quite hot. The country offers a range of climates that comfort its citizens and visitors. Israel offers extensive opportunities for a variety of experiences.

The diverse population offers a distinctive cultural dynamic, with an influx of ideas from the surrounding countries and peoples of the Middle East, as well as a wealth of culture from across the world, brought back to the land of Israel by Jews scattered during the diaspora. The traditions of countless areas, cultures, and cuisines have made their way to this country, and combined with the ancient traditions of the land. Add to this a strong desire to establish a modern nation, and you have the fascinating expression of a contemporary Israeli culture that blends the best of the world, both yesterday and today. Art, food, dance, performance, literature, and academia all flourish here, and offer so much to explore for visitors.

For families, Israel has more to offer than could be contained in the pages of any book, though this book will do its best to deliver highlights and help you to create a memorable experience for your family from the myriad opportunities for fun, adventure, education, exploration and family growth this great nation has to offer. There is a reason this land is so beloved by so many people. Let its beauty and exuberance open up your family to exciting new ideas and create memories to last a lifetime.

Some Basic Facts About Israel:

- **Population:** 7,821,850 (July 2014 est.)
- **Area:** 20,770 sq km total (20,330 sq km land and 440 sq km water)
- **Border Countries**: Egypt, Jordan, Lebanon, Syria
- **Religion:** Jewish 75.1%, Muslim 17.4%, Christian 2%, Druze 1.6%, other 3.9%
- **Language:** Hebrew, Arabic, English (most commonly used foreign language)
- **Capital City:** Jerusalem (population 829,000 in 2014 est.)
- **Other Largest Cities:** Tel Aviv-Yafo 3.559 million; Haifa 1.09 million (2014 est.)
- **Currency:** New Israeli Shekel (ILS)
- **Approximate Exchange Rate:** ILS per US Dollar = 3.908 (2014 est.)
- **Time Difference:** UTC+2 (7 hours ahead of Washington, DC, during Standard Time)

Information for US Embassy in Israel:

Address: Ha-Yarkon Street 71, Tel Aviv-Yafo, 63432, Israel
Phone: +972 3-519-7475
Website: http://israel.usembassy.gov/

US Consulate in Jerusalem:

Address: Agron Street 18 Jerusalem 9419003
Phone: +972 2-622-7230
Website: http://jerusalem.usconsulate.gov/

Why We Wrote This Book

Why we wrote this book is very similar to why we launched RealFamilyTrips.com. Born of the belief that travel is an important part of the family experience, a tool for both growth and fun. It exposes children to new ideas and educates them about the world. It provides opportunities for family bonding that are without compare. By showing your children new people, and ideas, as well as the wealth of history, you harness the past and the present to provide for their future.

We don't believe that "big trips" are something to be put off, or saved until children are "old enough" to appreciate them. Delaying these kinds of opportunities only delays their benefits. Our children surprise us with what they are able to absorb. Of course they may not remember every fact, every site or every detail of a trip when very young, but they will remember how it *feels*. This sensation experienced during great family travel is the part that is really transformative; the power to set a precedent that will follow them throughout their lives. The qualities of worldliness, thoughtfulness and curiosity are bred in children and nurtured through travel.

As amazing as it is, we also recognize that for a busy family, vacation can seem like anything but when parents consider the amount of effort, research and time that go into planning a great getaway. That is why we created Real Family Trips, and why we wrote this book. Our goal is to provide you with a definitive and informative guide, to save you the hassle of planning a trip so you can get on with enjoying it.

We curate days that provide a mixture of what every great vacation needs: opportunities for education, relaxation, excitement and family time. We select great places, great vendors and memorable experiences. We place an emphasis on realism, and would never recommend anything we wouldn't personally do, or anything that we know can't realistically be accomplished with several kids in tow.

It is our belief that a great trip requires context and information to accompany it. We encourage you to read sections of this book with your children before departing. Read from the daily introduction while in country, as you make your way from the hotel to your first destination. Emphasize to your children not only what you are seeing, but why. To understand the background, the culture, and the history of what you are seeing and doing is to give it importance and make the most of your experience.

We wrote this book because it is what we would want to have for our family vacations, and now we want to share it with you. We hope you enjoy this trip and those to come in the future. Cherish this time and make the most of your resources. Bon voyage, from our family to yours.

-The Team at RealFamilyTrips.com

Advice On Using this Book:

- The suggested vacation laid out in this book spans 12 touring days in Israel. It is designed so you can start on any day of the week and proceed in order from start to finish.

- This vacation, and the activities chosen for it, **works best in the summer.** While almost all of it is possible in the winter, and notations have been made when exceptions or changes apply, you will get the most out of this proposed itinerary during summer months.

- This trip works from front to back, beginning to end. At the same time, tastes vary, you may have already experienced some of these things in the past or may have different ideas. Appendix A in the back of the book contains some **suggestions for alternate activities**, as well as where they can be most easily swapped in to create a custom built experience for your family.

- All prices have been converted from ILS (Shekels) to U.S. Dollars. **These are approximations**, and based on exchange rates current to the spring of 2015. Exchange rates may vary slightly and/or vendors may change prices for your trip. These approximations are intended for informational purposes only.

- At the end of each day you will find **two sections labeled "logistics"**: a suggested order of the stops for that day (you can change it up if you like, our suggestions are based on ease of transportation and the creation of a cohesive day) and a list of clothing, sundries and other items you may need, or anything else to note and remember.

- We encourage you to read the accompanying children's stories. More about the stories on page 81.

- Finally, Appendix B at the back of the book, provides **additional resources**, including links from us to even more itineraries and ideas for things to do in Israel.

Advice On Enjoying Your Trip:

- Most of the days laid out in this proposed vacation are active and fairly busy. They allow a family to enjoy a wide variety of exciting and educational opportunities. However, if you aren't a "let's pack it all in" kind of family, don't force yourself to follow a plan or itinerary that seems like too much for you. This is likely to backfire.

- Always allow some time for wandering, and you may just discover the unexpected. One day on a past vacation, our family had planned on going on a second hike. We got lost and could not find the trail. As we were about to give up and head back, we rounded the corner and found ourselves by a beautiful glacier-fed lake. Our kids decided to jump into the freezing cold water, clothes and all - we had a blast. This was one of the most memorable and fun parts of the vacation, and it was spontaneous and unplanned. Let those moments happen, and don't stress if something goes amiss with your plans.

- Leave some time to think about and absorb what you saw and experienced, without trying to rush the entire trip. Recap and debrief at the end of the day and during meals. It is absolutely worth sacrificing a stop if it means you have the time to make the other ones really count.

- Push your boundaries and explore things that might be out of your normal character. Immerse yourself in the location. Experience all that the destination has to offer, not just the "main" or "top" tourist sites. Feel what it means to belong there and enjoy the culture and local population.

- Don't follow an itinerary if it simply doesn't interest you. What others think is awesome may be boring to you. No matter how incredible someone says the view might be from the top of the mountain, if you hate hiking then don't do it. Read the planned itinerary and choose what you are interested in seeing. There are also alternate activities in the back (Appendix A) which you can mix and match with established plans to make a day that suits you. Don't be afraid to make changes to a plan to make it your own.

- Read the background information for each day and stop with your family to provide context for what you will see. This will help give more meaning to what you see, prepare you for the trip, and generate excitement. We recommend that you watch movies, film clips, or view other media related to Israel before departing to help prepare and inspire you for the vacation to come.

- Assign projects for the kids. Our kids have to research where we are going. They have been really creative in the past, including drawing a map of our location and identifying the closest Starbucks to our hotel and at each stop we made. The Starbucks was to ensure dad was well caffeinated during the trip. They had fun doing it and presenting it to us, and we had fun listening and seeing what they did.

- Remember the basic things while traveling. Not getting enough sleep or not eating regular meals and snacks can damage even the most well planned trip, especially when children are involved.

- Make sure that you allow extra time, and expect that you will run into some delays. Use these as an opportunity to explore your surroundings and take in the local culture instead of viewing them as a negative.

Have an Awesome Adventure!

Day 1 - Jerusalem

Begin your family journey in Israel with one of the world's most beloved cities. From antiquity through the modern age, Jerusalem continues to be at the center of the conversation as a nucleus of faith, politics, culture and thought. It is a sacred and cherished land for Jews, Muslims and Christians. It has been home to some of the most pivotal events of mankind and revered by all who have lived in or visited it.

Today, Jerusalem serves as the capital city of Israel, and is home to the Knesset (Israeli Parliament) and other government centers. The oldest part of the city dates back more than 5,000 years and is considered one of the world's oldest cities, protected as a UNESCO world heritage site.

The Old City has been destroyed, besieged, conquered and has traded hands repeatedly throughout history. Despite having an area of less than one square kilometer, this oldest portion of Jerusalem houses multiple landmarks constituting some of the most sacred places in the world for a variety of religions. There is perhaps no place else on earth where the past comes alive quite in the way it does in Jerusalem. The passion that Jerusalem has inspired throughout history and into today is without equal. This will be increasingly evident as you walk the old city where you seemingly cannot take a step without bumping into another piece of antiquity.

This first day in Jerusalem offers a great way to dive into your exciting family experience. A mixture of history and exploration will provide context as well as excitement as you all warm up to this fantastic city and all it has to offer.

Get Oriented and Inspired - Wander through the old city and visit the Wailing Wall (Also Known as the Western Wall and The Kotel)

Jerusalem's Old City may be small, comprising an area of only about a third of a square mile, but its significance to both history and modernity is without parallel. This walled city holds some of the most important religious sites in the world for a variety of faiths: the Temple Mount and Western Wall for Jews, the Dome of the Rock and al-Aqsa Mosque for Muslims, and the Church of the Holy Sepulchre for Christians. The Old City is set inside a set of massive defensive walls, dating back to the 16th century and constructed by the Ottoman Empire. Today, it is roughly divided into four areas: the Muslim Quarter, the Christian Quarter, the Jewish Quarter and the Armenian Quarter.

Families will appreciate this section of the city for many reasons. Ancient architecture, narrow alleys, and colorful markets create an old world charm amid an otherwise modern city. You will feel as if you have stepped back in time and are walking through the past. The history of the city is mired in the complicated lore that Old Jerusalem has. Tragedies have affected this beloved city, but each time it has risen from the ashes and rubble. Today, one can see people of many faiths gathered and living together within the walls, and you can feel the power of the many sacred sites. The Old City offers hope for the future. Through the ages it has stood at the crossroads of the world, situated at the border between three continents. It has opened its doors for everyone from slaves and beggars to merchants and kings over the course of its storied history.

Travel Tip: Part of the charm of the Old City is the fact that so much of it remains untouched from ancient times. While this is a delight for picture taking and enjoying history, it can pose some challenges for strollers and those with limited mobility. Note that there are many steps, cobblestone stretches, or otherwise uneven streets and walkways.

While in the Old City, no stop would be complete without a visit to:

The Kotel - Western (Wailing) Wall

Phone: +972 2-627-1333

Website: http://english.thekotel.org/

This relatively small surviving portion of the western part of a barrier wall built to surround what Jews and Christians refer to as the Temple Mount, is a powerful site and an unforgettable part of any visit to Jerusalem. This western portion of the wall dates from the Second Temple period, and is considered the closest to the former Jewish Second Temple itself. This makes The Kotel the most sacred place in all of Judaism, and the location Jews turn to during prayer.

For centuries it has served as a place for pilgrimage by Jews, as well as people of other faiths. As stepping on the temple mount itself is forbidden, this closest remnant of the surrounding structure is used as a place of prayer and a strong connection to both the spiritual and cultural aspects of the Jewish faith. As a place of reverence, prayer is believed to have special weight when performed at The Kotel, as Jews recognize a divine presence here. The well known practice of inserting written notes of prayer into the wall is observed by some million or so people each year.

Many say that the action of visiting The Kotel, whether for a first time or a hundredth, is a moving experience despite the level of one's faith. Some say that they feel in touch with the divine here, while some may merely recognize the reverence in others and be moved by the passion that The Kotel instills. Visiting with an open mind and a respectful attitude will provide the best experience, and allow your family to define exactly what it means to you.

Please Note: Out of respect for the holiness of this site, the following should be taken into consideration. Modest dress must be worn to The Kotel, and men should cover their heads upon approaching (men can find cardboard skullcaps just before entering the actual area of The Kotel). On the Jewish Sabbath and holidays, electronic devices are prohibited in the area of the wall. Even those accustomed to different practices related to prayer and modesty at home should recognize the importance of adhering to the accepted practices at The Kotel and behave accordingly out of respect. Also, prior to entering the main plaza area of The Kotel, you will be subject to a security search which includes metal detectors and the examination of any bags. Please be aware and plan accordingly.

Travel Tip: We recommend making a second visit to The Kotel on Friday evening at sundown if you can manage it. This is when the Jewish Sabbath begins, and many Jews of all types come to pray their Sabbath prayers here. It is a beautiful sight and a powerful experience to share.

Explore History Together - Kotel Tunnel Tours

Besides the portion of the Kotel visible above ground, an extensive network of ancient tunnels, cisterns, aqueducts and other underground structures provide a direct link between the modern day and the Hasmonean period, dating back over 2,000 years. The tunnels that run approximately 488 meters along The Kotel provide a glimpse into history, as well as the unique architectural challenges that faced the construction of these magnificent structures.

Besides passing through archways and passages that support the wall and much of the city's Muslim Quarter, one of the benefits of exploring these tunnels is an opportunity to pass through and under the spot widely considered to be the closest one can get to the Holy of Holies. This is the location of the foundation stone and the single most sacred place for Jews, which cannot be directly accessed.

Between the opportunity to experience sacred ground, and the stones, models, and actual structures that provide insight into the construction of the Temple and builders of old - the Kotel Tunnel tour is not to be missed.

PLEASE NOTE: In order to access The Kotel Tunnels, you will need to be part of a guided tour. It is best to book in advance.

Approximate Length: 1-1 1/2 Hours

Approximate Cost: 5-10 dollars per person

Phone: +972-72-3290719

Hours: Sunday - Thursday, 7 AM - Evening. Friday, 7 AM - 12 PM. Closed Saturdays.

www.ibookisrael.com/tour/jerusalem/the-kotel-tunnel-tour

At this point we recommend stopping for lunch. There are a number of charming cafes and eateries in the Old City to please people of all tastes. Simply wander around and find a place that appeals to your family. This would also be a good time to do a little shopping in the Cardo area. This onetime main street of Jerusalem was originally paved 1,500 years ago by the Roman emperor Hadrian.

Today this mainstay of the Jewish Quarter has been rein-vigorated as a shopping district featuring art, souvenirs and various specialty goods. Occasionally, the area features theme days in which actors dressed in period costume offer explanations and activities for children.

Also Note: If you buy anything valuable, or larger than would fit in a locker, you should ask to leave it at the store, and return to pick it up after your upcoming visit to the Hezekiah Water Tunnels.The City of David (your next stop) is about a 10 minute walk back to the Cardo area, and a quick stop back will be manageable. Alternatively, you can easily come shopping here after the Hezekiah Water Tunnels stop, just note that you may be a little wet and dirty.

Wade Through the Past - Chizkiyahu (Hezekiah) Water Tunnels in the City of David

At the amazing City of David, your family can experience the ancient city ruled by King David. Located technically just outside the walls of the Old City of Jerusalem, this is the area written of in the Bible, the ancient land dating back over 4,000 years and containing archaeological elements from the First Temple Period and the world of Kings David and Solomon.

This impressive tunnel system runs over 500 meters into solid mountain, through a feat of ancient engineering described by an inscription near the entrance. Besides providing a glimpse into one of the oldest parts of Jerusalem, this tunnel system chronicles the efforts of King Hezekiah, as he ordered the tunnel dug so as to divert and protect the city's water supply during an incursion by an Assyrian army in the 8th century BC.

You and your family can trek through the tunnel, wading through cold, ankle to waist high water (depending on the season and your height) as you experience this ancient excavation and walk in the footsteps of history. It is a truly memorable experience, and while you get a little dirty and have to work at it a bit, the reward pays off with the feeling that you are walking on ground very few have had the privilege to explore.

Address: Hashiloach Road | City of David, Jerusalem, Israel

Getting Here: You can arrive after a brief, 5-10 minute walk from the Dung Gate, which itself is just a few minutes from the Kotel plaza (or a little longer from the shopping and eating areas of the old city).

Phone: +972 2-626-8700

Website: www.cityofdavid.org.il/en/tours/city-david

Hours: *Summer*, Sunday - Thursday, 8 AM - 7 PM. Friday, 8 AM - 4 PM. Closed Saturdays. *Winter*, Sunday - Thursday, 8 AM - 5 PM. Friday, 8 AM - 2 PM. Closed Saturdays. **Last Entrance to Tunnels is 1 Hour Before Closing.**

Approximate Cost: See website for information about tours and packages, or just admission to the area, depending on what you want to see and do.

Approximate Time: Depending on how many people are in the tunnel, and how rapidly everyone is making their way through, it can take 40-60 minutes to get through the tunnel.

PLEASE NOTE: A headlamp is a useful and inexpensive way to add to your experience here. You will see more and be free to explore with you hands, or steady yourself in the dark, uneven, and watery area. It will also come in handy over the course of your trip as other stops make use of one. The gift shop here also sells small lights as a backup.

Travel Tip: Many children absolutely love the water tunnels. However, some young children may be scared, as it is a long and very dark underground area. Our children have loved it since they were babies, but others have reported that their children found it too frightening. Also note that the water is cold, and on younger children it will come up quite a bit higher on their bodies.

Learn How it All Started - Herzl Museum

Theodor Herzl has been called the founder of modern Zionism, and was the visionary who made the modern state of Israel possible. An Austro-Hungarian author and academic, he promoted Jewish migration during the diaspora back to the land of ancient Palestine, and called for the formation of a

Jewish state. As the head of the first incarnation of the World Zionist Organization, it was Herzl who propelled the very notion of Israel to the forefront of world discussion.

The Herzl Museum chronicles the man as well as the mission, through a one hour audio-visual depiction of the Jewish world according to Herzl. It offers insight into the man and the process he went through, often difficult and tumultuous, to bring his ambition of a Jewish state into reality. Besides a unique glimpse at the life of a great man, the museum's tours and activities seek to bridge a gap between the historical and the present, providing a context for Israel and what Jewish values, vision, and imagination hold for everyone.

Address: Har Herzl neighborhood, Jerusalem

Getting Here: We recommend taking a taxi to the museum, or check for the available bus routes.

Phone: +972-2-6321515

Website: www.herzl.org/English/

Hours: Sunday - Wednesday, 8:30 AM - 6 PM (Last tour at 5 PM). Thursday 8:30 AM - 7 PM. Friday, 8:30 AM - 1 PM (Last tour at 12:15 PM).

Approximate Length: 1 Hour

Approximate Cost: $6.50 for Adults, $5 for Children (6+) and Seniors, Children under 6 are free with accompanying adult.

PLEASE NOTE: You *must* book in advance to guarantee entry, otherwise you will be limited to an as-available basis. The easiest way to do so internationally is by emailing the museum, museum@wzo.org.il

Ending the Day

At this point you will likely be tired. We recommend taking this time to head back to your hotel or other lodging, showering and resting up for a bit. Then, if feeling up to it, we advise heading to Ben Yehuda Street, also known as the "Midrachov" for dinner at one of the many restaurants and cafes there.

Logistics - Day 1

Suggested Order of Stops:

1. The Kotel/Old Jerusalem
2. Kotel Tunnel Tours
3. Stop for Lunch and Shopping in Cardo
4. Chizkiyahu Water Tunnels
5. Herzl Museum
6. Freshen Up/Grab Dinner

Things to Bring/Note:

- Modest clothing for The Kotel (but we recommend a change of clothes for the water tunnels)
- Comfortable, waterproof shoes for walking and tunneling. We recommend Keen water shoes, as they are comfortable for the tours and waterproof for the tunnels
- Consider leaving behind strollers
- Leave unnecessary bags behind to expedite security checks
- Headlamps for tunnel tours

Part I of the accompanying children's stories goes with today's itinerary and can be found on page 82. We recommend reading the story the night before, or morning of today's journey.

Day 2 - Jerusalem

Having established that Jerusalem is a city with a deep and powerful history, as well as significance to a variety of faiths, it is also important to see the ways in which it is a vibrant and modern city.

Modern Israel is alive and well, with a strong citizenship of Jews, Christians, Muslims, Druze, and others - who work together to build a strong community that celebrates itself, and is a major power on the world stage.

One could spend an entire lifetime studying Israel or even Jerusalem's past. Yet, it is also important to show children how the nation and the city function today. Your family will appreciate a chance to get a look at the inner workings of the city, learn about the politics and discussions being had today, and experience the diversity of the community at large here.

There are so many unique opportunities afforded by time in Jerusalem, a city which represents so much of what the world at large is experiencing right now. From commerce and industry, to politics and diplomacy, rich and poor, young and old, religious and secular - Jerusalem has it all and offers a very manageable slice of life that your family can experience in a relatively short time.

Of course, vacations should be about fun while away; but great vacations are also about enriching your lives for when you return. Open your eyes to the city and embrace all that is Jerusalem on this day in a city on the go, remembering its past and building for its future.

This second day in Jerusalem offers a variety of activities that allow your family to give back, to learn about the past and present, and to explore the diversity of the city. There are educational opportunities, "just for fun" stops, and many more that qualify as both.

Give Back - Volunteer at Pantry Packers

Part of appreciating what we have is giving back to those who do not. Just because you are on vacation doesn't mean there isn't time to help out. Teach your children crucial lessons in what your values mean to you.

Pantry Packers is the oldest continuously operated network of social services in Israel. The organization dates back to 1788, and ever since has been helping the poor, the elderly, and those most in need within the nation of Israel. At the Pantry Packers production facility in Jerusalem, tourists aged 8-80 are given a brief orientation session that includes watching a short movie, before donning gloves, aprons, and caps in order to fill bags of rice, beans, and other commodities. These bags, which bear a sticker with the name of the packing group, will later be included in large food baskets destined for needy families throughout the country. All the recipient families have been identified by government agencies as needy.

Pantry Packers is sponsored by Colel Chabad. This organization offers a complete range of social services programs to help Israel's neediest - including soup kitchens, aid for widows and orphans, pediatric dental clinics, immigration absorption services, Multiple Sclerosis therapy, bar mitzvahs for orphans, and programs for hospitalized children.

Please Note: Program participation must be scheduled in advance.

Team up with locals and other visitors as you help provide needed services to people who truly appreciate a helping hand. Too busy to stop in? Feel free to donate to the group as well.

Approximate Time: 1 1/2 Hours

Approximate Cost: Free of Charge

Address: Derech Moshe Baram | Jerusalem

Phone: (IS) 02-626-0035, (USA) 718-774-5446

Email: info@pantrypackers.org

Website: http://pantrypackers.org/

Interested? Sign up to Volunteer On Their Website

Unique Insight Into History - Visit Museum of Underground Prisoners

Located near the Russian Compound, this one of a kind museum offers insight into the formation of the State of Israel. While much of the story is known from actions and discussions that took place on the world stage, some of the battles to form the modern nation of Israel took place underground and behind the scenes.

This museum tells the stories of those who worked outside the public arena - Haganah, Irgun and Lehi - paramilitary and covert operatives, who played an integral part in the formation of the state.

The museum itself is located in a former prison operated by the British during the period of their mandate, adding to the air of what you will be learning here. Walk the ground where political prisoners were housed as you learn about those who sat among their ranks, as well as those who worked to free them and establish an independent Israel.

Among the exhibits, experience the prison cells, a bakery, a synagogue, the prison yard, a workshop, a memorial to the executed, and an "escape cell" - including a secret tunnel and a harrowing tale of a dozen prisoners who got out to join the War of Independence. While not a particularly pleasant atmosphere, this museum deserves a brief stop as it honors those who paid the ultimate sacrifice, and tells an important part of the story that made modern Israel possible.

Address: 1 Mishol Hagevura St. Russian Compound

Phone: +972 2-623-3166

Website: http://hamachtarot.blogspot.com/ (You will need to use a web translator if you do not read Hebrew)

Hours: Sunday - Thursday, 9 AM - 5 PM, closed Friday-Saturday

Approximate Cost: $4 per adult and $2 per child (up to age 18)

Approximate Time: 1 Hour

Explore Religious Culture - Wander the Mea She'arim Neighborhood

Mea She'arim is one of the oldest Jewish neighborhoods in Israel. The name loosely translates to "a hundred fold" and was so named for the weekly Torah portion read just after the founding of the community. It is an Ultra-Orthodox neighborhood, populated mainly by Haredi Jews.

A visit to this community offers a special opportunity to immerse yourselves in a strong religious and cultural presence. For the Ultra-Orthodox it may feel like coming home, and to others it likely will feel like you are stepping back in time.

Many of the original buildings remain, built in pairs facing each other across narrow courtyards and protective gateways. You'll enjoy a chance to browse religious bookstores and beautiful Judaica. If visiting on a Thursday or Friday, be sure to stop by the busy neighborhood bakeries, producing delectable challah and cakes for the Sabbath. Note that most stores will close early on Friday.

PLEASE NOTE: Modest dress is required in this neighborhood (skirts for women, with knees and elbows covered) and residents prefer not to be photographed. Please respect the wishes of the residents here and act accordingly.

Shop, Eat and Enjoy Like a Local - Pop by the Mahane Yehuda Market

Not far from the Gush Katif Museum (your next stop), is a great example of local commerce and culture in action. The Mahane Yehuda market, also referred to as "The Shuk", was originally an open air market, though it is now partially covered. Here you will find a little bit of everything, from clothes and accessories, to housewares, art and flowers. Then - of course - there is the food. Everything from fresh produce, meat, and fish to delicious baked goods, sweets, spices, halva, hummus, and exotic fare representing the diversity that is Jerusalem.

There are a variety of prepared foods that you can either buy from stalls or sit down and enjoy at a restaurant or cafe. Mahane Yehuda is a favorite among locals and tourists alike, and will afford your family a chance to dive into the scene while enjoying some delicious nosh in a uniquely Israeli venue.

The market dates back to the Ottoman period, when local peasants began using the once empty lot to sell food and wares, until it was eventually organized into a formal market. Originally a ramshackle initiative with no infrastructure, it grew through the period of British Mandate and on into independent Israel.

Today's Mahane Yehuda has developed into a modern and professional facility, while still maintaining old world charm and authenticity. It is the best of old meets new and a wonderful microcosm of the greater Israeli experience. If you like, you can look into tours here, or download a map in advance of your visit to plot your own route. You may also want to consider the "Shuk Bites" card offer. For about $26 per person, you get a sampling of some of the best the market has to offer and the opportunity to shop, tour, and taste at your convenience.

Website: www.machne.co.il/en/

We recommend stopping for lunch while at the market, to re-fuel and enjoy the delicious offerings before continuing on with your day.

Learn About More Troubled Times - Visit the Gush Katif Museum

While there is so much in Israel to celebrate, and so many tales of happiness, there are also examples of the times which have troubled the nation and given pause to its people. Gush Katif was a bloc of settlements in the Gaza Strip. Following a cabinet decision, the 8,000+ residents were forcibly evicted by the army in 2005.

The disengagement, proposed by then Prime Minister Ariel Sharon, represented a pullout from an area within the Gaza Strip - believed by some to be untenable in future and permanent definitions of the borders of Israel, and to open the doors for a peace process.

This museum tells the story of Gush Katif, from the building of the first home to the final expulsion. The exhibits include pictures, Torah scrolls, and other artifacts from Gush Katif. Admission also includes a film about life and industry in Gush Katif, as well as life for its residents after.

The museum is recommended for ages 7 and up, and parents should be aware that some subject matter is a little difficult. While there is an effort to remain neutral, there are inevitable political undertones families should be aware of. Settlements are an often controversial, but also integral, part of the story of

Israel. A full understanding of the modern nation should include a discussion of Gaza and the West Bank and those who settled there, despite any personal feelings on the matter. This fascinating look at the lives of the men and women living on the edge, quite literally, of Israel is a powerful, fascinating, and important stop.

Address: Sha'arei Tsedek St 5, Jerusalem, Israel

Phone: 02-625-5456

Email: mgushkatif@gmail.com

Website:
www.gushkatif.022.co.il/BRPortal/br/P103.jsp?cat=8771

Hours: Sunday - Thursday, 9 AM - 5 PM. Friday 9 AM - 1 PM. Closed Saturdays.

Approximate Cost: $5 per person

Approximate Time: 1 Hour

Learn From an Expert - Talk About "Israel Today" with Gil Hoffman

Gil Hoffman is the chief political correspondent for the Jerusalem Post. With great insight into the state of modern Israel and all the wonders it encompasses, as well as challenges it faces, he is a uniquely qualified speaker and guide.

Gil will speak about news, politics, and pressing issues in Israel today, as he shares insight with your family regarding the current state of affairs and next steps for the nation. While learning about the past is key, this unique glimpse at the political landscape through the eyes of a journalist will take you into Israel's present and provide a fuller picture of the nation. Special insights and the opportunity to ask questions and engage will provide the best chance for you and your family to understand the complexities of the modern Israeli scene, and leave feeling a deeper connection to what affects the country.

The talk can be conducted in your hotel lobby, a coffee shop or another location you designate. Gil and Fun In Jerusalem (the company who books his appearances) will work with you to create a custom experience that caters to your family, and focuses on the reasons to be optimistic about Israel's future. Sessions can be conducted in English or Hebrew.

Approximate Length: 1 Hour

To Book This Experience: visit www.funinjerusalem.com/ or email them, info@funinjerusalem.com.

Wind Down and Get Crafty - Take in Hutzot Hayotzer

Hutzot Hayotzer is a lane dedicated to arts and crafts in Jerusalem. Located just west of the walls of the Old City, here you will find artists set up and displaying their wares, with some of the most fun and unique art the city has to offer.

This will be a special treat for children, as they will enjoy not only getting to see the colorful crafts but getting up close and personal with artists, some of whom work right on the lane itself. Hutzot Hayotzer means "the creator steps out", a name that says it all: artists out among the people, sharing their craft and their gift with the world.

If you visit in early August, you are in for a special treat. The annual Hutzot Hayotzer Fair is an all out bash that Jerusalem looks forward to all year. Whether you choose to buy something, or simply enjoy wandering and interacting with the artists and viewing their amazing creations, your family is sure to love the extra flair the festival brings.

The fair also brings food stalls, workshops for kids, and open air concerts - featuring some of the best musical talent in Israel. Everything stays open late during the festival and artist demonstrations as well as the shows will continue on until your family is ready to stop.

Grab some dinner at Hutzot Hayotzer and enjoy the festive atmosphere until you are ready to retire for the night.

Logistics - Day 2

Suggested Order of Stops:

1. Volunteer at Pantry Packers
2. Museum of the Underground Prisoners
3. Mea She'arim
4. Lunch and Explore Mahane Yehuda
5. Gush Katif Museum
6. Political talk with Gil Hoffman
7. Take in Hutzot Hayotzer/Possibly the Fair
8. Dinner around Hutzot Hayotzer

Things to Bring/Note:

- Comfortable shoes for walking
- Modest clothing for Mea She'arim neighborhood
- Don't forget to give the kids some snacks and fuel up at Mahane Yehuda, a great place to nosh

Part II of the accompanying children's stories goes with today's itinerary and can be found on page 87. We recommend reading the story the night before, or morning of today's journey.

Day 3 - Tel Aviv

Tel Aviv is Israel's "city by the sea." This picturesque metropolis sits on the Mediterranean coast and boasts high rises scattered amongst lower level developments and beachfront establishments. The first thing that will strike you after leaving Jerusalem behind is that this is most certainly not a city built thousands of years ago. Cut stone and cobbled streets are swapped out for concrete and steel. Tel Aviv is a contemporary city, and a nod to the Israeli desire to marry the ancient with the modern.

While seemingly polar opposite from Jerusalem, the fun of Tel Aviv is noticing the through-lines that make Israel neither beholden to its past, nor ignorant of its future. Here, religious sites are swapped out for nightclubs and beachfront resorts. A liberal attitude replaces solemn deference, yet it is still a city in which Jews - and the other religions and cultures that make Israel what it is - come together and celebrate their heritage, while building a unique vision for the future.

You will also find that Tel Aviv is generally more relaxed than Jerusalem. Absent here are religious neighborhoods in which special dress is required. Quite the opposite, it seems everyone in "TA" is casual and milling around looking for the next bit of fun and excitement.

Take a cue from these locals and enjoy being a little less touristy and a little more family on the hunt for fun. You'll enjoy a relaxing pace and a friendly atmosphere as you dive further into Israel and expand your understanding of the sheer variety that defines the nation and its people.

This day in Tel Aviv has your family finding some time to learn, but also to relax and enjoy a very different vibe as you see more of the broad spectrum that Israel has to offer. Celebrate the differences that make this city, and each of its inhabitants unique. Now is the time to cut loose a little and have fun in the sun, the Tel Aviv way!

History With a Tel Aviv Twist - Tour the Palmach Museum

Before slipping fully into "beach bum" mode and literally kicking off your shoes, take advantage of one of the great educational opportunities in Tel Aviv with the unique experience of the Palmach Museum.

The Palmach was a military strike-force of the underground Haganah defense organization (which you learned about just yesterday in Jerusalem). This group, which predated the modern state of Israel, would later be integrated into the Israel Defense Forces. They represent an important component of the military force that made modern Israel possible, and represent extraordinary individuals with unique stories.

To pay homage to the uniqueness of these soldiers, and to show you the difference between Jerusalem and Tel Aviv, this museum takes a radically different approach. The "experiential" museum sees you and your family "join" a group of young recruits upon enterring. You then proceed through from the establishment of the unit, through the end of the War of Independence.

There are no traditional exhibits here, as you forgo displays and artifacts for a hands on account of the events, as told by documentary materials including three-dimensional decor, films, and various special effects. The result is a much more personal and hands-on recounting of events as you are thrust into the middle of the story.

This museum tells an important chapter in history, and does so in an innovative way that is, itself, telling of Tel Aviv and the type of modern thinking that abounds here.

Address: 10, Haim Levanon Street, Tel Aviv, Israel

Phone: +972 3-545-9800

Email: palmach_reservation@mod.gov.il

Website: www.palmach.org.il/Web/English/Default.aspx

Hours: Sunday - Friday, by pre arranged visit ONLY. Email them to book.

Approximate Cost: $8 for Adults, $5 for Children

Approximate Length: 1 1/2 Hours

Ages: 6 and Up

Some Artsy Flair - Visit the Nachlat Binyamin Crafts Fair

Twice a week, local artists set up shop along Binyamin Street, one of the longest in the city, and take it over in an explosion of color, patterns, fun, and excitement. To visit on any other day and return during the fair, one would have trouble recognizing the street. Over 220 artists on average gather to put on demonstrations, hawk their wares and create a festive atmosphere for locals and tourists alike.

The biggest event of its kind in Israel, you can find everything from jewelry and ceramics, to toys, paintings, Judaica, and all manner of specialty items and fun tsotchkes. There are rather strict rules, ensuring that all items are made by hand and that the actual artist, not a representative, is present at the stall. All artists are hand selected and meet a rigid set of criteria. In other words, this is all quality merchandise. You will also find street performers, fortune tellers, clowns and other sights to delight children and get everyone in on the fun. All the goods are as unique as the fair itself. This is sure to create a lasting memory and be a favored part of your time in Tel Aviv.

The street itself is charming and also features many established cafes and restaurants if you are uncomfortable trying your hand at street food. Just go with the flow here, and whether you buy something for yourself, a gift to bring home, or choose to just take in the scene and enjoy the energy, this unique venue is sure to win you over.

Address: Nahalat Binyamin Street, Tel Aviv-Yafo, Israel

Email: info@nachlat-binyamin.com

Website: www.nachlat-binyamin.com/en-Default.aspx

Hours: Open Tuesdays and Fridays (and many holidays) from 10 AM - 6 PM (7PM in July and August)

We recommend stopping for food as you explore the fair, and eating up before taking your time at the next stop.

Sand and Sun - Relax on a Tel Aviv Beach

At this point in your day and your vacation as a whole, it is time to enjoy some well deserved relaxation and let the kids be kids on a beautiful, lively beach. Featuring almost 9 miles of beachfront land, Tel Aviv has a sandy spot for every family and something to suit all needs.

Most beaches offer chairs for rental. There are also bathrooms and showers in most beach areas, and besides the waterfront cafes and restaurants, you will also find vendors walking around with cold drinks and sundries. If you don't feel like sitting still you can also find water sports and plenty of action like parasailing, kayaking, boogie boarding, volleyball, and more.

"Matkot" is the favored beach activity, a game involving wooden paddles and a small ball. You'll hear the distinct "crack" of the ball smacking the paddle up and down most beaches. Many have designated areas for the game, away from sunbathers and diners. If you want to "go local", find a game and join in!

If you need a break from the beach you can also stroll the boardwalk. This promenade, or "tayelet", features food and drink, shopping, artists, street performers, and other fun diversions for when you want to stay in the sun but take a break from the sand.

There are 16 designated beaches in total, each with a slightly different flair and to suit different tastes. **Tel Baruch Beach** is a good option for families, as it is clean and well kept, with a small bay that keeps the waters calmer for small children. **Metzitzim Beach** is more family oriented in the north, with a children's playground and family vibe, while the south half is more for teens and 20 somethings looking to play Matkot and unwind in their own space. This may be a good option for families with a variety of ages who need a little space to spread out and be independent. The religious beach **Hof Hadatiyim** caters to those who need to follow strictures related to separating men and women.

Logistics - Day 3

Suggested Order of Stops:

1. Visit to Palmach Museum
2. Explore Nachlat Binyamin Craft Fair
3. Lunch at or near the fair
4. Relax on One of Tel Aviv's famous beaches

Things to Bring/Note:

- Comfortable shoes for walking
- Towels and bathing suits, sunscreen and other beach essentials

Part III of the accompanying children's stories goes with today's itinerary and can be found on page 92. We recommend reading the story the night before, or morning of today's journey.

Day 4 - Northern Israel

Northern Israel, including the Galil and Golan areas, repre-sents some of the most stunningly beautiful and relatively un-touched land in the entire nation. Israel shares its northernmost border with Lebanon and Syria, and the area just south of this border is primarily agricultural. Here lie Isra-el's most fertile and favorable land for farming, and the locals take advantage of this fact as they produce some of Israel's most abundant crops, as well as local wines, dairy, and other delicacies.

Tourism here is a more recent development, with much of it tied to the agriculture of the area. Here you will find food and wine tours, as well as adventurous activities for families open to them, and scenic grottoes or vistas that celebrate the un-touched land and its natural charm. Camping is abundant in this region, as are opportunities to "rough it" with barbecues, cookouts, hiking, and the like. You'll find such other fun activi-ties as water sports, rock climbing, and extreme sports to break up some of the denser or more serious days devoted to spiritual learning or historical education.

While there may be less education in play here than ancient Jerusalem or modern Tel Aviv, this is still Israel, and Talmudic sights as well as biblical places of importance are scattered about - though they may have more distance between them than in urban settings.

The North will offer a nice change of pace, and break up your family's vacation with opportunities for the kids to let loose, as well as the adults. Bond over excitement and physical activity in a truly beautiful setting.

This day in Northern Israel offers a great mix of activities. Have fun with animals and set the pace for your Golan adven-ture with some great action, but also gain context for the area by learning about it firsthand. Exercise mind and body as you push out of the city and stretch your legs in the wide open Israeli air.

Get Situated for the Day - Drive from Jerusalem (or wherever you chose to stay the previous night) and arrive in the north of Israel.

Depending on your exact point of origin and destination, we estimate about 2-3 hours from Jerusalem, less from points north of the city.

You can choose to find a driver to take your family the distance, or rent a car . The latter option will allow you more mobility in the area (which will have less public transportation) and a way back.

Family Fun With Nature - Monkey Forest in Yodfat

Yodfat is a is a moshav shitufi (a sort of cooperative village, not unlike a kibbutz) in the Lower Galilee, south of Carmel, Israel. Founded by students in 1960, it borrows its name from a Second Temple era town of the same name, which was located in the region. This modern village was built by Jews of traditional values, in an attempt to preserve culture in a way that serves as an archetype for much of what modern Israel stands for. Today the community is comprised of around 160 families, with many working in agriculture, but also representing an expanded notion of the original communal founding.

The Monkey Forest is an animal shelter and educational tourism venue that brings you and your family up close and personal with a variety of amazing creatures. For 45 years, the facility has evolved from a relatively simple petting zoo, to a force in tourism and education. Today, the children of the area are the ones who are responsible for the care and needs of the animals, and this is extended to your children upon visiting, allowing them to get close and establish a real connection with amazing animal life. The goal is not only to teach important facts about animals, but to instill values of love, care, and compassion for all creatures of the earth and nature as a whole.

Here you will find multiple types of monkeys, as well as donkeys, ponies, goats, turtles, bats, snake, deer, gazelle, and a variety of exotic birds on top of assorted indigenous wildlife.

Your family will enjoy the opportunity to walk through scenic forest trails, meet the animals living in this natural habitat, and even stop for a picnic along the trails as you commune with this setting.

Please Note: One of the things that makes this facility unique, besides allowing you to walk freely among the animals, is that at the present time, they allow you to feed many of the animals by hand with food brought in. There are strict rules about what foods are allowed (and acceptable options for purchase on the grounds) and these feeding rules, as well as general rules of conduct, are very important for both adults and children to read, understand, and adhere to.

Email Address: monkeyforest.y@gmail.com

Phone: 04-9801265

Website: www.kofim.co.il/#!home/c1556

Hours: Sunday - Thursday, 9 AM - 4 PM. Friday, 9 AM - 3 PM. Saturday, 9 AM - 4 PM.

Approximate Cost: About $9 each for children and adults, 20% discount for seniors and special needs, 10% discount for students. You should try to book in advance, which is most easily done from abroad by emailing them.

Approximate Time: 1-2 hours

You'll want to take your lunch here in the picnic area within Monkey Village. Enjoy a nice picnic with the family as monkeys run overhead for an experience you will not soon forget.

A Deeper Understanding - Lebanon Border and Israeli Defense Forces Jeep Tour with Israel-Extreme

Travel through the sweeping mountain terrain at a brisk pace made possible only by being in the care of those who know it best. Take your newfound knowledge of the IDF and see soldiers and veterans in action as they show you the incredible beauty of the north firsthand. You'll enjoy panoramic views of the Kinneret and the spectacular Galilee landscape, spread out before your eyes.

You'll drive through running rivers (depending on the season) as you hear about the history, geology, and local plant and animal life from those who know it best. You will get a solid dose of excitement as you ride across the rugged terrain in an army jeep, while still expanding your knowledge of the area and gaining further context for its importance to the state of Israel.

With this touring opportunity, you can get up close and personal with the Lebanese border in eastern Galilee, where the Malkiya Kibbutz is located. This collective, almost as old as the nation itself, was founded by demobilized soldiers in 1949.

According to Israel Extreme, this is a tour not offered in other guidebooks or official tourism channels. A local guide from Malkiya will join the jeep tour and guide your family on a unique excursion through the eyes of a Kibbutz farmer.

This journey "behind the scenes" offers a view of life along the Lebanese border, "an ordinary life under threat." Your family will learn about what it takes and means to live life along a sometimes volatile border. You will learn about the geopolitical realities of the region and gain further knowledge by hearing about it first hand - from active duty soldiers engaged in the day to day defense of the border. See them in action (not combat, but in uniform and on patrol) and there is even a chance your family may get to climb onto a tank.

The tour will also take you through orchards and fields to experience kibbutz life firsthand, viewing the fields from scenic viewpoints. Depending on the season, you may have a chance to help plant a tree near the border fence, or taste local fruit (in the summer and fall). Further developing your idea of life on the border, you will visit the bomb shelter of the local kindergarten. All of this will provide your family with a better understanding of the conflict, the lives of the soldiers, those they protect along the border, and everyday life on a kibbutz in a way that will allow your family to see both staunch differences and striking similarities to your own lives. These are people just like us, ordinary people living under extraordinary circumstances, and this very special tour will instill a healthy understanding of this in children.

Approximate Time: 2-3 hours, depending on what you choose to do and local variables.

Contact: Interested in this tour? Book through Israel-Extreme (and be sure to let them know you are a friend of RealFamilyTrips.com)

Website: www.israel-extreme.com

Reference: Sima Sharabi

Office Phone: 04.666.9965

Email: info@israel-extreme.com

Go Local - Wander Around Tiberias and Find Dinner

Tiberias is a city in the north, located on the western shore of the "Kinneret", which is what Israelis call the Sea of Galilee. Dating back to the Roman Empire, this stunning example of Lower Galilee is truly something to behold.

Tiberias has a storied history and spiritual significance. Historically it served as the largest Jewish city in the Galilee, and a hub of religious and political thought. It has also been known for its hot springs for thousands of years, which are believed to have restorative properties.

Today, it serves as a lively city for tourism, with a variety of activities, as well as opportunities for shopping and dining, and attractions for all ages. The city is also host to a variety of hotels of different types. Enjoy a relaxing family dinner with stunning views of the Kinneret as a nice way to wind down your day.

Logistics - Day 4

Suggested Order of Stops:

1. 2-3 Hour Drive to Northern Israel
2. Monkey Forest in Yodfat
3. Lunch at Yodfat Picnic area
4. Lebanese Border Tour
5. Explore and Grab Dinner in Tiberias

Things to Bring/Note:

- Looser clothing for a warmer, more active day

- Comfortable shoes for walking

- Small, natural foods for feeding animals in Yodfat

- *The following recommendations are made by Israel Extreme for the day's adventures with them:*

- A driver's license is A MUST! Without it you cannot drive

- Closed shoes and long pants (not a must, but recommended)

- Camera/Video

- Sunglasses

- Sunscreen

Day 5 - Northern Israel

Still in the stunning, majestic locale that is northern Israel - with stunning views of mountains and fields, glittering green treetops framed by azure blue skies - it is time for your family to really appreciate the uniqueness of this setting and the opportunities it provides.

Any good family vacation involves some opportunities to learn and expand your understanding of the world around you. Similarly, there should be some time for casual relaxation and unwinding. We believe that another component that families need to pay attention to is FUN!

While there is much to learn in this part of the country, consider this day an opportunity for good old fashioned fun and excitement. Help your family appreciate the great country of Israel by doing some things that, while not necessarily unique to the country or inherently Israeli, will create the sort of amazement and adrenaline-pumping excitement that will forever tie Israel to great times for all of you.

This recommended day of adventure and exploration will surely leave a mark on your family, and may just be the thing you run home to tell all your friends about after the trip. At the same time, it may not be for everyone, in which case we point out that Israel Extreme offers a variety of off-the-beaten-path activities for a variety of tastes. Don't like climbing? Dive into local cuisine or explore on a walking tour. We also remind you that at the end of this book we have recommended some great alternate activities that may better suit the needs of your family.

This day in Northern Israel is all about getting your heart pumping with one-of-a-kind offerings from Israel Extreme. This tour company specializes in excitement and family activities that inspire you to think outside the box of what a "normal" tour of the country has to be (HINT: It doesn't *have* to be anything, just exactly what you want it to be!).

Extreme Family Adventure - Rappelling, Big Swing, and Spelunking

Alma Cave offers a chance to experience Israel from a new point of view. It is one thing to take in the beautiful sights of the Galilee and Golan Heights, it is another thing to do so while hiking, swimming, and climbing your way across Northern Israel with a company that can help you get the most out of the experience.

Enjoy a scenic view of Mt. Hermon, the Golan Heights, the Hula valley, and Mt. Evyatar as just part of the panorama you will enjoy from an angle few others see, and all of which you will appreciate in a fresh light thanks to the context provided by previous days.

This day of adventure **lasts 4 1/2 to 6 1/2 hours** though there are opportunities for breaks and you can turn back at any point for any reason.

The activities will be broken into 3 separate adventures:

Rappelling:
After a brief, 5-10 minute hike from where you park your car, you will suddenly arrive at the opening in the ground that leads to breathtaking Alma Cave. At this point, your family can enjoy the views and get excited for the climb as your guide sets up the ropes. You then have a chance to rappel down the side of the cliff and into the entrance of the cave. The air will be cool and the view stunning as you feel like real life adventurers and explorers.

Big Swing:
Upon entering the cave and disengaging from your ropes, each member of the family will have the opportunity to be harnessed into another rope, that offers a horizontal, "Tarzan-style" swing through the open air of the cave. You'll enjoy the rush and special take on this massive underground space as you fly through the air in a very thrilling experience that offers great family fun.

Spelunking:
Also known as cave diving, is special way to enjoy this awe inspiring locale and all it has to offer. You will begin with a short hike in the vast underground area using headlamps. You will then climb up and down ladders, and follow your guide as you pass through cracks in the rocky outcropping on an adventure children will get a real thrill out of.

TRAVEL TIP: A headlamp is really necessary. While you can *technically* use a flashlight, a headlamp is recommended as you will see more and be free to explore with you hands, or steady yourself in the dark, rocky area. It will also come in handy over the course of your trip as other stops make use of one.

ALSO NOTE: All of these activities are optional, so if children are too young or if they (or the adults for that matter) feel uncomfortable they can opt out of any of the activities while still participating in the day. The cave portion may be a bit challenging at times, so you should also know that it follows a back and forth route so you are never "trapped" or "too far" to go back. You can ask to turn around to make sure everyone remains comfortable and happy. **Also, no climbing experience is necessary**.

Consider a Different Kind of Accommodation - Camp Overnight with Israel Extreme

If your family truly is the adventurous type, and are willing to try a different sort of experience, consider staying overnight with the folks at Israel Extreme for a unique camping experience under the starry skies of Northern Israel. You can negotiate this when you plan your trip with them, but basic amenities include the following:

- Tent, Sleeping Bag and Air Mattress
- Guide to Stay Overnight with Your Family (they set everything up and take it down)
- Campfire Set Up By Your Guide

You can also add a very special barbecue dinner, in which food and preparation are provided. There are two price levels for the dinner, which include slightly different foods, all of which are details you can arrange with Israel Extreme.

About The Company - Israel Extreme:

Israel Extreme's focus on customer service means that you'll get a hands on experience creating your own package, and a chance to tailor activities for the specific makeup, abilities and demeanors of you and your children. Choose from a wide array of activities including spelunking, rock climbing, bungee, zip-lines, rappelling, skydiving and more. They also offer water sports like kayaking, active pursuits like hiking and horseback riding, as well as jeep tours, ATVs, and paintball.

Their specialty options mean you can work in educational opportunities as well, ranging from archaeology, holy sites, nature and antiquities, to "just for fun" options like winery tours for adults, or Krav Maga classes for all ages.

Their guides are well versed experts, who can teach you while keeping you engaged. They have guides that speak English, Russian, French, Spanish, German, Yiddish, and Hebrew.

Prices depend on a variety of factors, including the number of people and the specific activities. Options for meals include the outdoor barbeque, catered meals, restaurant stop-offs, or snacks for any level of adventure package. Mention RealFamilyTrips.com and you may receive consideration in pricing.

Contact them today to begin planning your trip:

Website: www.israel-extreme.com
Reference: Sima Sharabi
Office Phone: 04.666.9965
Email: info@israel-extreme.com

Logistics - Day 5

(Order of Stops Will Be Provided by Israel Extreme)

Things to Bring/Note:

- Comfortable Clothing for Athletic Pursuits as You Climb and Swing

- Headlamps for Caving

- *The following recommendations are made by Israel Extreme for the day's adventures with them (in addition to the headlamps, which they recommend):*

- Hiking boots or other sturdy, closed shoes. Sneakers are fine. Basically they just need to be strong, closed shoes. Water shoes, Crocs, and sandals are not sturdy enough

- Camera

- Drinking Water - at least 2 liters per person

- Sun hat, sunglasses and sunscreen

- Lunch and snacks

- Back Pack with two shoulder straps for carrying everything with your hands free

Day 6 - Northern Israel

After enjoying a day of fun and excitement, as well as the possibility of sleeping under the wide open skies of northern Israel, your family should be well acclimated to the area.

While clean air, gorgeous views and green pastures never get old, this last day in the North before heading back to a more urban setting will change things up some, and afford your family new opportunities to bond and explore.

Having enjoyed the stunning mountains of the Golan Heights from the very top of its spires to the bottom of its caves, today you explore the water. With the Sea of Galilee to the East, and Mediterranean to the West, the Galilee is surrounded by stunning bodies of water that are best experienced firsthand.

Take to the water with your family, and experience the old world charm of historical coastal cities to round out your vision of the region and provide a further understanding of the character that makes Israel what it is, as well as what it was throughout the ages.

Start your day with more adventure, of a slightly different variety, from Israel Extreme. Then continue on for some more history and exploration as you make your way back towards Jerusalem, and say goodbye to the north, but not without some fun and fanfare.

One More Extreme Activity - Rappelling at Keshet Cave

Some would call this point the most beautiful view in Israel, high praise for a country that offers so many treats for the eyes. Once an actual cave, this rocky structure has partially collapsed over time (don't worry, it is stable now) and only a stone archway remains, lending the site its name. Many millennia have shaped this point which is flanked on one side by the glittering waters of the Mediterranean Sea, and on the other by the entirety of the Galilee. Once you catch your breath from the stunning visuals, your family will begin a guided adventure, rappelling off the gigantic stone arch between two mountains. You will take to the air, only increasing your appreciation for the amazing panorama.

The 35 minute hike back up is a bit strenuous, but the use of cables will ease the strain as you continue to find new angles from which to admire the land and sea. Who knows, you might even encounter a curious mountain goat or two on the way back up!

According to Israel Extreme, the site is accessible to all, even strollers and wheelchairs. All the "extreme" activities are optional, and you are again provided with the choice to pull out at any point. No experience is necessary, and it is said that the rappelling is easy as you are not actually facing a rock cliff, but aided in an open air descent by the staff.

Approximate Time: 2-4 hours

PLEASE NOTE: This, like all extreme adventures, varies in cost and if this particular activity does not interest you it can be substituted for others found on the Israel Extreme website. Plan your package by sending them an email. Remember to mention RealFamilyTrips.com for possible consideration in obtaining a discounted price.

Take to the Water (With Speed) - Tornado Boating at Rosh HaNikra

Rosh HaNikra, or "head of the grottoes", is another jewel of Israel located in the north. For some of the best in Israeli seaside sites, look no further than this stunning geological formation on the coast of the sprawling Mediterranean. Enjoy blue waters as far as the eye can see, as you then gaze up at the white chalk cliffs adorning the land of Western Galilee. The cliff face opens up into spectacular grottos formed by the mighty sea beating back at the cliffs over the ages.

Your family will have the opportunity to enjoy these views from one of the most modern and powerful boats around. The "Tornado" boasts two 70 horsepower engines that get the boat up to speeds of 45 knots. Trust us, this is fast. The inflated rubber ship cuts through the surf as you enjoy the sea breeze and light splash of the cool waters as you swiftly jet through the sea spanning the rugged northern coast between Achziv and the cliffs of Rosh HaNikra, along the Lebanese border.

The outing is coordinated with the Israeli Navy for safety purposes, and an Israeli military ship will be on guard throughout the adventure to allay any concerns over safety. This pulse pounding activity will create exciting memories on the water, and provide still further insight and another angle from which to view this beautiful part of the country.

Age Limit: Minimum age is 5; there is no maximum age

PLEASE NOTE: This, like all extreme adventures, varies in cost and if this particular activity does not interest you it can be substituted for others found on the Israel Extreme website. Plan your package by sending them an email. Remember to mention RealFamilyTrips.com for possible consideration in obtaining a discounted price.

Approximate Time: 2 Hours

ALTERNATE: Take to the Water (At a Slower Pace) - Kayaking at Rosh HaNikra

Families who want to experience the majesty of Rosh HaNikra - and the soft chalk cliffs worn away by time, which demonstrate how both man and nature have literally shaped the land of Israel - have another option. You may prefer a slower pace, want to be more actively involved in your adventure, or you may simply enjoy the prospect of some exercise. For you, we recommend kayaking with Israel Extreme.

The total length of the grottos runs some 200 meters, with plenty of opportunities to branch off in different directions, push into some of the water caves, and traverse interconnecting segments.

Once upon a time, the only access to these majestic grottos was from the sea, and only experienced divers were able to admire their beauty. Today, a cable car can lower you to the ground level, where you then start from the beach, cross open water all the way to the caves, and come as close as possible to the Lebanese border. Push into the caves and admire amazing, natural geological formations in the limestone, and admire this calm respite amid the busy sea.

Just as with the Torpedo boat, the Israeli Navy will be alerted to the outing and have military personnel keeping a close eye.

Recommended Age: 10 and up

Approximate Time: 2 Hours

PLEASE NOTE: This, like all extreme adventures, varies in cost and if this particular activity does not interest you it can be substituted for others found on the Israel Extreme website. Plan your package by sending them an email. Remember to mention RealFamilyTrips.com for possible consideration in obtaining a discounted price.

Ride and Learn - Rosh HaNikra Cable Car and Walking Tour

As part of your day with Israel Extreme, you will have the opportunity to see the grottos from another angle. Ask about their cable car ride and walking tour, an opportunity to slow down to a pace where you can really learn about the fascinating science behind these soft chalk walls and cavernous natural structures. See them from above as you take a slow, relaxing cable car ride down from the top to the bottom, and let knowledgable guides instruct you as you see the same formations you took in from the water in a new light. This chance to catch your breath and explore will be a nice change of pace, and lend context to the day's activities at Rosh HaNikra.

Shop and Explore - Akko (Acre) Old City and Market

To say Akko is a story rich in history would be the understatement of the century, or rather, the last 50 centuries. As one of the oldest continuously inhabited sites in the region, Akko traces its roots back to the early Bronze Age, or about 3,000 BC.

The fascinating history of the city provides a unique blend of east and west, not unlike Jerusalem or Istanbul. It has long served as a crossroads for the world, played host to a variety of religious beliefs and practices, as well as elements from a wide variety of ancient and contemporary cultures. From the Canaanites to the Romans, the Byzantines, the Crusaders, the Mamluks and the Turks, on to the British - many have had a stake in this beautiful city over the ages.

Simply walking the old city, you will have an authentic look into the past, as the buildings tell their own stories. Vast fortresses and castles, stunning synagogues, mosques and churches, as well as other structures - tell the story of a city that many have lived in, loved and fought for through the ages. Among these are remnants of the Hellenistic and Roman periods, as well as structures from the Crusades and the Ottoman Empire. Be sure to look out for the underground Crusader city, Khan al-Umdan, the Turkish Baths, the Baha'i Temple (this is the holiest city in the world for the Baha'i faith), the Ramchal Synagogue, and the Citadel of the Knights Hospitaller.

Today Akko features markets sprinkled between old city walls, museums, and even modern touches like relaxing beaches and watersports for those looking for a bit of excitement. The coastal location means a vibrant seaport for fisherman. If the timing is right, you might even catch a street fair or festival to add to the excitement of this city and all it has to offer.

Spend as much time as you like, remaining conscious of the drive ahead. It is easy to get lost in enjoying Akko and let time slip away from you, there truly is so much to see and to do.

Back to the Big City - Car Ride back to Jerusalem

At this point it is time to bid farewell to the Galil and Golan and head back to Jerusalem to spend the night and begin anew the next day. **The car ride should be about 2 to 2 1/2 hours** back from Akko, possibly a little less. We recommend stopping along the way for dinner.

Logistics - Day 6

Suggested Order of Stops:

1. Rappelling at Keshet Cave
2. Tornado Boating **OR** Kayaking at Rosh HaNikra
3. Grab lunch in Rosh HaNikra
4. Cable car and walking tour at Rosh HaNikra
5. Explore City of Akko
6. Drive back to Jerusalem

Things to Bring/Note:

- Clothes that can get wet for boat trip
- Possibly a change of clothing for the second part of the day, if you think you might get uncomfortable
- Things to keep the kids happy/entertained on a 2 hour or so car ride
- *The following recommendations are made by Israel Extreme for the day's adventures with them:*
- Back Pack with two shoulder straps for carrying everything, so that your hands will be free.
- Hiking boots or other sturdy, closed shoes. Sneakers are fine, but hiking boots are best. Water shoes and sandals are not sturdy enough.
- Camera
- Drinking water - at least 1 1/2 liters per person.
- Sun hat, Sunglasses and sunscreen
- Wet Wipes - your hands and shoes may get dirty

- Lunch and snacks, or stop for lunch along the way.

- No specific clothing needed for either boating adventure, but keep in mind you could get wet. **Please note that for any electronic devices you should bring a protective bag or covering**.

Part IV of the accompanying children's stories goes with today's itinerary and can be found on page 97. We recommend reading the story the night before, or morning of today's journey.

Day 7 - Jerusalem/Dead Sea

With a healthy exposure to the majesty that is Jerusalem, it is time to see the city in a new light. Great family vacations have something for everyone, and while visiting the landmarks and exploring as a family are important, offering something specifically on your children's level will be key to not only having the kids enjoy themselves, but making sure that they walk away with an understanding of the city.

Jerusalem's central location makes it an ideal stage from which to launch an exploration of the surrounding area, which contains some important sites and fantastic opportunities for family growth and bonding.

Good fun, great meals and a chance to take a dip in one of the world's most famed bodies of water will all cement the earlier memories you have of Jerusalem. Further expand your vision of this city as not only a part of history, or a modern metropolis, but a vibrant community where family values shine and there is a lot to enjoy for people of all ages.

This day in Jerusalem and its environs includes a fun mix of activities that will create lasting memories for children. Take the opportunity to grow closer to your kids, and bond as a family. See it as a chance to "team up" with Israel, as a great nation unites with great parents, to provide children with the time of their lives.

A Unique Way to Explore - Scavenger Hunt in Nachlaot

Nachlaot is a cluster of small, courtyard neighborhoods in central Jerusalem. The area is categorized by narrow, winding lanes and charming, old-style housing with a small town feel amidst the backdrop of the big city. Described as one of Jerusalem's "best kept secrets", this colorful area serves as the perfect setting for family fun.

Try your hand at something different, with an activity filled morning from Israel ScaVentures. These family scavenger hunt activities are prepackaged and prepared so that all you have to do is show up and enjoy. They supply maps, mission packs and source sheets that serve as your guide to a fun, fascinating, and activity filled time in the city of Jerusalem. You will also have an Israel ScaVentures guide with you (not just the material) to facilitate the experience. Work together as a family, as you navigate streets and alleys, markets and neighborhoods, learning as you go.

This is a great way to learn more about the city in a unique way, with a whimsical sense of purpose as you explore with the intent to solve the puzzle rather than just wander aimlessly. You'll also appreciate the opportunity to work as a team, growing closer to your children as you unite to hunt down Jerusalem's hidden treasures.

Like the idea but not sure about the location? The company offers other routes in Jerusalem including the Old City Scavenger Hunt, Yemin Moshe Scavenger Hunt, City & Shuk Dash or the Watchman Scavenger Hunt, designed for those with an interest in Christian sites.

Address: (You'll get a meeting point when you get your confirmation details, varies some with the hunt you choose)

Phone: Tali, 0528-358-072

Email: tali@israelscaventures.com

Website: www.israelscaventures.com/

Approximate Time: 2 Hours

Approximate Cost: Quoted price is $311, for a group of up to 15. Price can vary for bigger or smaller groups, contact them to check current pricing.

Travel Tip: Since you will be in the area of Mahane Yehuda, we recommend popping in for a quick lunch. If not there, you will also find plenty of other eateries in the area.

Enjoy Nature's Spa - Mineral Beach at the Dead Sea

The Dead Sea (also known as Salt Sea) is a natural salt lake bordered by Jordan on the East, and Israel on the West. Located over 1,400 feet below sea level, high salt content (over 9 times that of the ocean) in the water allows the body to naturally float . This is a quintessential Israeli landmark and a must-visit spot when touring the country.

The location has been revered throughout history, serving as a refuge for King David and one of the world's first health resorts (for Herod the Great). For ages it has been a supplier of mineral, health and beauty products; including salt used in Egyptian mummification, potash for fertilizers throughout the Middle East, and a source of salts, herbal sachets, and mineral rich mud shipped around the world.

Mineral Beach, located on the northern shores of the Dead Sea, serves as a top destination for relaxation and therapy. Cover your body in some famous dead sea mud, soak in a therapeutic sulfur pool, and wash it all off with a serene dip into some of the most famous waters in the world.

Use this as a chance for your family to kick back and take in the natural offerings available at mineral beach. Children will enjoy bobbing along in the water and the unique properties of the great salt sea.

TRAVEL TIPS:

1. *If you or your children have cuts or bruises, the water will sting due to the high salt content.*

2. *Do NOT get any of the water in your eyes, for the same reason.*

3. *Generally, most beaches here are not "luxurious" and can be a little gritty, but it is worth the experience.*

4. *DO put mud all over (except your eyes) and have fun with it!*

PLEASE NOTE: You will see that on Day 8 of this proposed trip, we recommend visiting Fox's Chimney, which is located in the Dead Sea area. While it may be more logical to enjoy this relaxing stop at the Dead Sea on Day 8, the choice was made based on the fact that our Fox's Chimney stop is in the evening. Feel free to adjust your schedule to suit your own preferences, and also see our alternatives for the Dead Sea area in Appendix A. In the summer months, Fox's Chimney can also be visited at sunrise. If you and your family are early risers, you can visit the Dead Sea after your early morning experience at Fox's Chimney on Day 8.

Getting There: Mineral Beach is located approximately 1 Hour outside of the city of Jerusalem. We recommend renting a car for at least the day, in order to easily find your way here, to have a change of clothes with you, and in order to facilitate a stop on the way back.

Phone: +972-2-9944888

Email: avic@m-shalem.org.il

Website: www.dead-sea.co.il/en/

Hours: Sunday - Thursday, 9 AM - 5 PM. Friday, 9 AM - 4 PM. Saturday, 8 AM - 5 PM.

Approximate Cost: Adults are $16 weekend/holiday, $13 weekday. Children over 6 are $9 weekend/holiday, $8 weekday. Children under 6 are free.

Take a Unique Meal - Dinner at HaCnaanite Meat Bar & Restaurant

On the way back to Jerusalem from the Dead Sea lies a unique and dining experience. HaCnaanite features sweeping views of the Judean desert, while offering a slice of the past with delicious and authentic cuisine.

Located in the Nahal Prat, overlooking the Good Samaritan Ridge, this location serves as a literal desert oasis, offering good food and fun in the Judean Desert. Meals are cooked to order in an authentic brick taboon oven, right in front of your eyes. The restaurant believes in local sourcing of produce and all the meat is spiced and flavored with these regional flavors. The restaurant specializes in smoking and grilling special cuts of meat.

Take in a rustic, small village vibe with their outdoor dining - it will allow your family to feel as if you are dining in some biblical locale. Take in the sunset with the majesty of Israel as a backdrop, and authentic cuisine to complete the special atmosphere.

There is a kids menu available and accommodations can be made for groups. Enjoy your meal as long as you like, the longer portion of the drive back to the city is behind you, with only 15 or 20 minutes to get back to Jerusalem after the meal.

Address: Kfar Adumim Junction, Jerusalem

Phone: 02-535-5351

Hours: Sunday - Thursday, 6 PM Until Last Customer. Closed Friday and Saturday.

Getting There: Drive on Route 1 back from the Dead Sea towards Jerusalem, turn at the Kfar Adumim sign. Public transportation is also available.

Logistics - Day 7

Suggested Order of Stops:

1. Scavenger Hunt in Nachlaot

2. Relax at Mineral Beach, Dead Sea

3. Optional: Ein Gedi, Water Hike. (See Appendix A at End of this Book)

4. Dinner at HaCnaanite Meat Bar & Restaurant

Things to Bring/Note:

- Comfortable clothes and shoes for running around during scavenger hunt

- Bathing suits, towels and beach gear for Dead Sea visit

- Change of Clothes for Dinner

- Easiest to have a rental car for today

Part V of the accompanying children's stories goes with today's itinerary and can be found on page 101. We recommend reading the story the night before, or morning of today's journey.

Day 8 - Jerusalem/Dead Sea

A great family vacation is all about working around any idea of a "regular" schedule in order to seize opportunities as they come. It is also important to build in enough time to relax, to ensure you are sleeping right and to wander, shop and enjoy an area at your own pace. If you aren't taking a breath you are probably missing something.

Spread throughout the city of Jerusalem are some great neighborhoods to wander and explore, to shop and eat, and to focus a little less on tourism and a little more on letting the moment take you away.

It is also important to note that some activities can only be done during the day, but it would be a shame to overlook those that occur at night as well. In order to fully experience the area, it is a good idea to mix up your timetable a little, in order to experience both morning and evening activities. With some careful planning, this can be achieved without running yourselves ragged, or pushing children too far.

This day, partly in Jerusalem, lets you sleep late, in order to keep moving later. Explore different parts of the city, before you head back to the Dead Sea for more excitement with Israel Extreme. Explore a shopper's paradise and a fascinating cave all in the same day!

PLEASE NOTE: There is an entire alternate plan for this 8th Day of travel, located at the end of the book in Appendix A. This alternate day forgoes the return to the Dead Sea in favor of more rappelling and caving adventures in the Central Israel area. Take a look and decide which best suits your family.

Get a Late Start, On Purpose - Sleep In and Catch Up on Rest

In order to keep yourselves moving late into the day, to enjoy a fantastic evening activity, allow yourselves to sleep in a little. About halfway through your trip, everyone is most likely more than ready for some extra R and R, so embrace the opportunity to take your time this morning and sleep soundly.

Retail and Relaxation - Brunch and Shopping at Mamilla Mall

As part of a "lazier" morning, enjoy a chance to wander and shop in one of Jerusalem's premier retail areas. Mamilla Mall is a shopping district near the entrance to the Old City of Jerusalem. It is comprised of an open air promenade lined with charming stores and cafes, as well as a two story indoor complex with more chances to eat and browse.

Considered a more upscale shopping district, you'll find a lot of quality wares here. There will be outposts for many popular, international brands you'll recognize from home, as well as some unique and inherently Israeli stores and art galleries. The fact that most of it is open-air helps it feel less claustrophobic, and maintains some of the charm of the area, rather than simply feeling as if you are in another mall back home.

Take the time to sit and relax at one of the many cafes for a leisurely brunch. There is no rush today, and the charm of eating a late morning meal while looking out on the Jaffa Gate and Tower of David will be a special treat.

TRAVEL TIP: If shopping isn't your thing and you are eager to get back to visiting historical sites, or if you simply want to break up the morning's retail adventure, several historical sites have been incorporated into the mall complex in the interest of historical preservation. Here you will find the Clark House, Convent of St. Vincent de Paul, and Stern House.

How to Get Here: Next to Jaffa Gate, at the entrance to the Old City & from the bottom of King David Street. Accessible by Buses 13, 18, 01.

Phone: 02-6360000

Website: www.alrovmamilla.com/

Hours: Sunday - Thursday, 10 AM - 10 PM. Friday, 9:30 AM - 2:30 PM. Saturday, 1 Hour from End of Shabbat - 11 PM.

Some Key History - Visit the Israel Museum

Given a chance, a visit to the Israel Museum is a must for any family. The Israel Museum is the largest cultural institution in the State of Israel and is ranked among the world's leading art and archaeology museums. Founded in 1965, the Museum is celebrating its 50th anniversary in 2015, with many special exhibitions and loans from Museums around the world. With over 500,000 objects in its permanent collection, the Israel Museum's holdings are encyclopedic - housing some of the most prized artifacts and works of art found in Israel. On the way in, enjoy views of the Knesset and the Israeli Supreme Court.

This modern and thoroughly professional venue was completely renovated in 2010 and houses materials from prehistory on to the present day. The Museum is divided into five wings: Archaeology, Fine Arts (where you'll find such impressive and famous works of art as Camille Pissaro's The *Tuileries Gardens, Afternoon Sun* and Sunset at Eragny), Jewish Art and Life, a Youth Wing (which includes two fantastic exhibitions that are really well suited for kids and families) and the Shrine of the Book - home to the Dead Sea Scrolls. The 20 acre campus also boasts the beautiful Billy Rose Art Garden, with famous sculptures throughout.

The museum is best known for being the home of some truly unique pieces of history, offering a slice of a variety of cultures and religions. Among these truly special exhibits are a carved female figurine considered the oldest artwork in the world, the interior of a 1736 synagogue from Suriname, a mosaic Islamic prayer niche from 17th-century Persia, and a nail used in crucifixion during the time of Jesus.

While one could easily spend a whole day (or more) here, we recommend focusing your trip on 3 main exhibits that are incredibly important, and lend background and context to the rest of your visit:

1. Model of Jerusalem from the Second Temple Period.
2. The Dead Sea Scrolls, housed in a special, dome shaped building, the Shrine of the Book.
3. The Archaeology Wing tells the story of man, from the prehistoric era through the time of the Romans.

While you and your family can feel free to explore as much as you like, these three stops represent some top highlights that children will be interested in, and will allow you to keep moving and make the most of the remainder of the day.

Address: Derech Ruppin 11, Opposite the Knesset, Zip: 9171002

Phone: +972 2-670-8811

Email: info@imj.org.il

Website: www.imj.org.il/en/

Hours: Sunday - Monday and Wednesday - Thursday, 10 AM - 5 PM. Tuesday, 4 PM - 9 PM. Friday/Holiday Eves, 10 AM - 2PM. Saturdays and Holidays, 10 AM - 5 PM. (During July and August, the Museum is open late on Wednesdays. Please check the Museum's website before you visit.)

Approximate Cost: $14 Adults, $7 Children. Children are FREE on Tuesdays and Saturdays.

TRAVEL TIP: Tickets can be purchased in advance, this allows you to avoid waiting on line and get in quicker. Do this before you leave home and print them out for the simplest experience.

Also Note: There are two kosher dairy cafes (Mansfeld) and one meat restaurant (Modern) on the premises, as well as a smaller café (not kosher) near the entrance to the Shrine of the Book.

Early Nosh and More Free Time - Wander and Grab Dinner on Ben Yehuda Street

Also known as "Midrachov", Ben Yehuda Street joins with Jaffa Road and King George Street to form the Downtown Triangle, a central business district. It has been a main street and popular thoroughfare since before Israel became a formal nation.

Already having had an experience with the area on your first day, it provides an opportunity to wander and shop a little if you choose, or to simply have an early bite for dinner at one of the many great restaurants. After you eat, take a chance to freshen up at your hotel if you like, and prepare yourself for a great evening activity.

PLEASE NOTE: Depending on the pace your family moves at, and what you like to do (and if you opt for the sunset or evening version of the next stop), you may not be able to fit everything in today. Mamilla Mall and Ben Yehuda Street both offer shopping and eating opportunities and if you feel time is tight, we recommend choosing between the two.

Underground Under the Stars - Underground at Fox's Chimney

Now is the time to depart from Jerusalem and head back to the Dead Sea area. This will take about an hour to an hour and a half, whereupon you will again meet up with Israel Extreme. Start time is around 7 PM, travel by highway on route 1 to route 90.

This whole day has been leading up to one unforgettable experience, and the shift in time was with a good reason. You will link up once more with Israel Extreme in the early evening, because this activity is simply too hot to enjoy during the day. You begin with a hike of about 45 minutes to an hour, marching from the banks of the Dead Sea to the rare majesty of Fox's Chimney. On the way, enjoy beautiful dusk views of the Moav Mountains, Edom, and the Dead Sea. The hike is on the challenging side, but according to Israel Extreme, children as young as 4 can handle it provided they are active and generally up for physical activity.

Fox's Chimney is one of only a few salt caverns in the entire world. Here you will enjoy another rappelling adventure, this time into the crystalline beauty of a salt lined cavern that stretches deep below the center of the earth. All in all, you'll descend around 210 feet below the surface, enjoying spectacular views all the way. Once you reach the cavern floor, the real fun begins as you marvel at salt and rock formations, enticing stalactites and stalagmites, and rich bands of salt encrusting the earth's deepest nethers. Enjoy a true caving experience as you navigate narrow crevices to reach spectacular open chambers.

This is a truly unique, once in a lifetime excursion. You'll see things few others have ever gazed on, and enjoy one of the rarer natural formations on earth. The adventure is well worth planning your day around, and will bring you closer as you all pick your jaws up off the cavern floor together.

Contact: Interested in this tour? Book through Israel-Extreme (Remember to mention RealFamilyTrips.com for consideration in obtaining a discount)

Website: www.israel-extreme.com
Reference: Sima Sharabi
Office Phone: 04.666.9965
Email: info@israel-extreme.com

TRAVEL TIP: As an alternative to the evening hike and climb, you can opt to do this trek at sunrise or sunset as well. For the sunrise excursion you start early (meet at 4:45 AM) and finish around 10 AM. The sunset hike meets at around 5:30 PM. It is less hot at those times, and Israel Extreme recommends opting for either sunrise or sunset for the best possible view. We have chosen the evening time for a less impressive panorama, but a more convenient time. In the non-summer months, there are some daytime options allowed for by cooler temperatures.

Logistics - Day 8

Suggested Order of Stops:

1. Late Wake Up and Collect Yourselves for a Big Night
2. Leisurely Stroll, Shopping and Brunch at Mamilla Mall
3. Visit Israel Museum
4. Wander and Grab an Early Dinner on Ben Yehuda Street
5. Travel to Dead Sea Area
6. Caving at Fox's Chimney

Things to Bring/Note:

- If you bought tickets in advance for Israel Museum, don't forget to bring them with you in the morning
- Good, athletic clothes for climbing
- Headlamps for caving tour
- Easiest to have a rental car for today

Day 9 - Gush Etzion and Nitzanim

Gush Etzion *is a cluster of Jewish communities located in the Judaean Mountains and south of Jerusalem and Bethlehem. The core group of agricultural villages and settlement communities were built in 1940-1947, on land purchased in the 1920's and 30's. Many were subsequently destroyed in the War of Independence and rebuilt after the 1967 Six-Day War.*

The establishment and protection of West Bank settlements is a key part of Israel's history and identity. No telling of the story of this nation and its present day circumstances would be complete without learning about the settlements, and no trip to the region would be complete without a visit.

The kibbutz is a uniquely Israeli vision, a type of collective community founded on a mix of socialist and zionist ideologies that have formed a special identity and a powerful part of the Israeli experience. In the beginning, they were primarily agricultural collectives, but as the nation and its people have evolved so have the kibbutzim. Today they represent forays into industrial and high tech sectors, while still maintaining deep roots in tradition, and the ideals of those who carved the nation of Israel out of rock and desert.

This day, just south of Jerusalem, will show your family a slice of Kibbutz life and a step into the past, with a chance to bake traditional bread and learn about a different side of Israel than you have seen previously. End the day relaxing on an idyllic beach for a day that is fun, as well as indicative of the rich traditions of the land.

A Tradition of Making - Bread Baking Workshop at Pat Bamelach Artisan Bakery

Promoted as "Connecting to Israel and Classical Jewish Sources Through Bread", this unique workshop offers so much in a single activity. There is education, both historical and cultural, combined with culinary exercise and a tasty pay-off at the end. While other sources may offer similar experiences, we recommend booking through www.FuninJerusalem.com.

This hands-on foccacia bread workshop has you and your family rolling, kneading, shaping, seasoning, and baking in a traditional brick oven. The workshop takes place in the bakery and under supervision from professionals, including Rabbi David Katz.

Along with the bread baking and tasting, a conversation led by Rabbi Katz will accompany your time here. You can choose one of the following topics for an in depth take, or opt for a brief overview of all of them:

1. History of Bread in the Bible and Jewish Law

2. The Grain Cycle and Holidays in Israel

3. From Harvest to Sacrifice - how grains and breads were used in the time of the Jewish Temple

Extras are also available (for an additional cost) which include: a full breakfast spread (egg salad, tuna salad, cut veggies, fruit salad, cold drinks, hot drinks) to accompany the bread, honey tasting and talk (if during the honey season), gluten free or non wheat flours if your family prefers or someone has a dietary restriction.

PLEASE NOTE: All workshops require advance bookings, pat@funinjerusalem.com.

The workshop takes place at Rosh Tzurim in Gush Etzion. This religious Kibbutz in the West Bank was established in 1969. The name, roughly translated to "Top of the Rocks", originates from a Biblical passage in Numbers, and also refers to the beautiful views from the Judean Mountains.

The kibbutz, established by Bnei Akiva Religious Scouts and Nahal soldiers, was founded on a rich sense of religious deference and tradition. Today, they raise turkeys, produce milk, and grow grapes for wine production, along with other fruits and crops. Your family can be a part of their rich tradition for a day, as you engage in a time honored practice that will also promote family togetherness.

Address: Rosh Tzurim, Israel

Email: patbamelach@funinjerusalem.com

Website: www.funinjerusalem.com/pat-bamelach/

Approximate Length: 1 1/2 Hours

Approximate Cost: Varies with size of group and length of time, as well as selection of any extras.

A Different Sort of Beach - Family Fun at Nitzanim Beach

In case your time in Tel Aviv didn't cement the idea for you, going to the beach is something of a national pastime in Israel. With 70% of citizens living on or near the coast, this is a country that enjoys their fun in the sun. Having gotten a taste of the more cosmopolitan beaches of the city areas, take some time to enjoy this unique setting, in a quieter part of the country.

Nitzanim Beach, located mid-way between Ashdod and Ashkelon, is one of the best stretches of coastline Israel has to offer, and a well kept secret to boot. The nearby kibbutz of the same name, is the site of quite a bit of history of its own. Founded by immigrants, many of them Holocaust survivors, Kibbutz Nitzanim was bombarded and captured by the Egyptian army during the 1948 Arab-Israeli War in the Battle of Nitzanim. A nearby memorial, called Andarta La'lochemet Ha'Ivria, pays homage to the women who fell during this time of conflict.

The beach features showers, a place to change, restrooms, and a restaurant that offers light refreshments. Just before arriving at the actual beach, to the right, is a small pond outfitted with pedal boats that you can rent. This is sure to be a winner for small children, as you can meander around the lake, taking in the scenery and splashing about. You can also choose to hop out and take a "hike" in the pond, wading through the water at your own pace.

Travel Tip: Waterproof shoes or sandals will be a plus for either the paddleboats or the "hiking." Again, we recommend Keen water shoes. You should also note that the paddleboats are a spring/summer activity, and as early as September the off season will see them out of service.

Approximate Cost: $8 per car on weekends, $6.50 on weekends

Logistics - Day 9

Suggested Order of Stops:

1. Bread Baking Class at Rosh Tzurim
2. Nitzanim Beach

Things to Bring/Note:

- Bathing suits, towels and beach gear for beach
- Water Shoes/Sandals for Pond
- Easiest to have a rental car for today. **PLEASE NOTE:** Some rental car companies may restrict you from driving in this area. Please check with your rental company before you drive here, and as another option, you can always hire a driver.

Day 10 - Mitzpe Ramon

Having had a chance to enjoy the big cities of Jerusalem and Tel Aviv, as well as rural life in the agricultural north, it is time to turn south, to the majesty of the sprawling Negev Desert. Taking its name from the Hebrew word meaning "dry", the Negev represents more than half the country.

While there is much to see in the south, including Kibbutz Sde Boker, to which first Prime Minister David Ben-Gurion retired, as well as his namesake University - much of the charm lies in experiencing the smaller communities of the Negev.

You could venture to the large administrative capital of the district at Beersheba, or the tourist mecca and resort locale of Eilat, both of which have much to offer visitors. However, we recommend Mitzpe Ramon, a smaller town (population around 5,000) full of charm and opportunities for eco tourism and history, both regional and national.

Founded in 1951, Mitzpe Ramon emerged first as a community for the workers building the road to Eilat. It became a permanent settlement, falling on hard times for a period as Israel rapidly expanded, but once again came into its own as a burgeoning population became interested in exploring the land within Israeli borders. Jeep tours, hiking, nature sports, and active pursuits became a local industry and reestablished Mitzpe Ramon.

Local highlights include the Ramon Crater, the zoological garden, and cultural fixtures like the Mitzpe Ramon Jazz Club and The Adama Dance Company. The area boasts a number of places to stay including the Beresheet Hotel, as well as a Bedouin inn and a large number of quaint bed and breakfasts.

This day in Mitzpe Ramon allows you to see the beauty of the Negev, while taking you through some other local highlights. Get active, see some animals and appreciate the beauty of life outside the city in a unique venue that lends itself to hiking, camping and communing with the Israeli countryside.

A Scenic Drive - Make Your Way South to Mitzpe Ramon

It is time to strike out from the big city once again, and make the drive south to Mitzpe Ramon. You'll want to leave early to make the most of the day, between 8 and 9 in the morning. Taking route 40, largely considered a more scenic and enjoyable route south, will get you where you need to go, while providing a great view of the desert and parts of Israel that will be sure to delight children.

Renting a car for this journey makes far more sense than trying to find a driver for the 2 1/2 hour trek. It will also afford you more mobility in the area and help you get back to the city after day 11 (this is an overnight journey to Mitzpe Ramon).

Tour With an Expert - Ramon Desert Tours

Mitzpe Ramon is a perfect launching point for an exploration of the Negev, a region characterized by beautiful desertscapes and wild, untouched nature. Authentic Jeep tours, like those offered by Ramon Desert Tours, are a great way to make the region accessible for all ages, and can be combined with a variety of other great activities.

A guide is essential here, as navigating the vast desert terrain will be almost impossible on your own, and a guide helps the subtle nuances of history and nature come alive. Adding in other, exciting activities will help keep children engaged and make for a magical day in the Israeli south.

We recommend the following activity with tour guide Oded, if interested, you may be able to book more or different activities through him:

Rappelling:
Located on the edge of the Ramon Crater, Mitzpe Ramon is perfectly situated for some amazing rappelling adventures. After getting oriented and seeing a bit of the area, let your guide bring you to the southern part of town, past the hotels and campsites, to the cliffs. Here you'll get to experience the rush and see the sites as you rappel down and get a pulse pounding start to your day here. Although we featured rappelling adventures during the trip up to northern Israel, to rappel here is to experience it in a new way, with new views and a very different experience. At the same time, if you feel it is too much for your family, you can see other ideas in Appendix A. **Approximately 90 minutes.**

About The Company - Ramon Desert Tours:

Specializing in Jeep tours, Ramon Desert Tours has a variety of options including diverse trails and numerous possibilities to customize your experience. Whether you want to spend a few hours or a few days in the area, this Mitzpe Ramon based company will create an adventure to suit your family.

You can make requests, or choose from a list of great extras that include rappelling, hiking, camel rides, bedouin tea services, and so much more.

Their guide Oded has a wealth of experience and offers tours rich in knowledge as well as family fun. Keep your children on the edge of their seats, eagerly awaiting their next bit of desert adventure!

Prices depend on a variety of factors, including the number of people and the specific activities. Mention RealFamilyTrips.com and you may receive consideration in pricing.

Contact them today to begin planning your trip:

Website: www.ramontours.com/201041/English
Reference: Oded
Office Phone: 972-52-3962715
Email: odedbaba@gmail.com

Embrace the Desert Life - Camel Ride

Children of all ages will enjoy this opportunity to experience a slice of desert life that dates back through the ages. Hop onto some of these storied beasts of burden as you bob along the desert landscape and hear about life in the Negev. This will be a great photo opportunity for your family, and create a lasting memory for children as they get up close and personal with animals, and enjoy a camel-eye view of the area just like the ancients did. **Approximately 30 minutes.**

Various locations in and around Mitzpe Ramon can facilitate camel rides for you and your family.

Learn More About the Area - Mitzpe Ramon Visitor's Center

The visitor's center offers a one hour, self guided tour that will provide an overview of the area and context for your visit. Learn about the diverse local ecosystem, and enjoy stunning views of the crater and all that it holds. Also here is the Ilan Ramon memorial, a tribute to Israel's first astronaut. After some great outdoor time, this respite will give you a chance to catch your breath and expand your knowledge of the Negev and Israel. **Approximately 60 minutes.**

Address: Ma'ale Ben Tur Street 1, Mitzpe Ramon, Israel

Phone: +972 8-658-8691

Website:
www.parks.org.il/ParksAndReserves/ramon/Pages/default.aspx#_=_

Hours: Summer, 8 AM - 5 PM except Fridays and Holiday Eves, 8 AM - 4 PM. Winter, 8 AM - 4 PM except Fridays and Holiday Eves, 8 AM - 3 PM

Approximate Cost: Adults $8, Children $4

Something Fun For the Kids - Trip to an Alpaca Farm

Time permitting, you and your family can spend time communing with these sweet and gentle creatures. While not native to Israel, these South American imports look and feel right at home in the Negev. Children, especially younger ones, will love the opportunity to feed and pet the animals, taking time to enjoy their company and celebrate the spirit of nature that is such an integral part of the community here.

Phone: +972 8-658-8047

Email: alpaca4@gmail.com

Website: www.alpacas-farm.com/#_=_

Hours: Summer, 8:30 AM - 6:30 PM. Winter, 8:30 AM - 4:30 PM.

Approximate Cost: $8 per person.

At this point we recommend returning to your hotel or other lodging to shower and have a nice dinner to fuel up for your next stop.

End Your Day Under The Stars - Stargazing with Ira Machefsky

Before an overnight stay in one of Mitzpe Ramon's beautiful hotels, or charming B&B's, spend some time admiring the natural beauty of the night sky. Now that you are far away from the big cities, the vast open skies of this desert community make for some of the best stargazing in Israel. Add to your appreciation of the stars by working with an accomplished and knowledgeable professional, who can guide you and your children to a greater understanding of the cosmos.

Known as the "Star Man of Mitzpe Ramon", Ira Machefsky has over 40 years of astronomy experience. His tours begin with a naked eye observation period, celebrating the clear skies over the Negev, in which the Milky Way is often clearly visible and the dark, relatively pollution free skies of Mitzpe Ramon see a night illuminated by a wide array of constellations. The second half involves a "portable observatory" as you and your children enjoy guided stargazing through telescopes.

Ira will help you and your children understand how the celestial sphere works, observe stars, learn their names, and understand stellar evolution. You will also have a chance to observe planets and their moons, star clusters, nebulae, and deep sky objects. As an additional treat, the tour offers a chance to hold actual moon rocks, as well as a 4.5 billion year old piece of cosmic history.

Ira will meet you at your hotel or you may have to follow briefly in your own car (another good reason to have a rental for today). Tours are not private, though they can vary widely in size. It may be up to 20 people or so, or may be just you and your family. It all depends on current demand. Chairs and blankets are provided for this night under the stars.

NOTE: No previous experience or knowledge of astronomy required. Recommended for ages 6 and up.

Address: 8 Nachal Grofit, Mitspe Ramon 80600, Israel

Phone: 1-972-(0)52-544-9789

Email: machefsky@gmail.com

Website: www.astronomyisrael.com/

Hours: Viewings occur daily, except Friday nights and Jewish Holidays. Sessions begin at 9:30 PM in the Summer, and 6-6:30 PM in the Winter.

Approximate Length: 2 Hours

Approximate Cost: $40 per Adult, $20 for child (age 6-12), no charge for children under 6. Maximum Charge of around $195 per nuclear family. **Israeli Shekels preferred, will take American or other currency in a pinch.**

Logistics - Day 10

Suggested Order of Stops:

1. 2-3 Hour Drive to Mitze Ramon
2. Rappelling and Touring with Ramon Desert Tours
3. Camel Ride
4. Visit Mitzpe Ramon Visitor's Center
5. (If Time Permits) Alpaca Farm
6. Shower and Stop for Dinner
7. Stargazing with Astronomy Israel

Things to Bring/Note:

- Looser clothing for a warmer, more active day
- Comfortable shoes for walking
- Rental car is a good idea for this excursion
- Plenty of bottled water for the day

Day 11 - Mitzpe Ramon

Mitzpe Ramon and the surrounding Negev represent an area of outstanding natural beauty within the south of Israel. The area is cooler than other parts of the Negev, due to its relatively high elevation over the nearby crater.

Ramon Crater, also known as a makhtesh, is approximately 25 miles long by 6 miles wide. It serves as home to an astounding array of local wildlife, including the curious ibex and a variety of birds and reptiles. While bearing some similarity to the arid regions of the American southwest, it is also a world unto itself. Clear, untouched stretches of desert lend an atmosphere of exploration and the allure of being a settler on the edge of civilization.

A Jeep tour offers your family the ability to cover large swaths of the desert landscape in a relatively short time - from the comfort of a vehicle - while still embracing the trailblazing nature as you bob along the dirt roads at brisk pace, enjoying the sun and cool breezes.

Having spent the previous day with some adventurous exploits, and the chance to learn about the area, today is all about diving in. Scenic views from the visitor's center are great, but the crater and the beauty of the Negev are best appreciated by getting up close and personal, under the care of a knowledgeable guide.

Enjoy a full day's tour of the Mitzpe Ramon area, including breathtaking natural features and a little local fare. Accompanied by Oded of Ramon Desert Tours, you will have a chance to see firsthand what you have been learning about, and have a true desert experience to bring your Israeli exploration full circle.

Full Day Experience - Jeep Tour with Ramon Desert Tours

Ramon Desert Tours offers a fully customizable experience, and provides your family with the ability to see as much or as little of the area as you like, with additional options to zero in on areas of nature, history, and culture that are of particular interest to you. Departing from Mitzpe Ramon as a home base, and getting you around by Jeep, their all ages adventures are the simplest way to maximize your time here.

You can work with the company to handcraft a trip for you and your family, starting from just a few hours. We recommend a full day tour here (approximately 9 AM - 5 PM) as less time will make it difficult to really experience all the area has to offer. There is some driving time in between sites, which aren't as closely packed together as they are in a city environment. By taking a guided tour, you ensure that even this time spent in transit is not lost. You have the opportunity to hear about everything you see, and engage a knowledgeable guide with questions to keep you children engaged and interested.

Just some of the highlights we recommend including in your day long tour are:

Makhtesh Ramon

Venture into the crater itself to get up close and personal with its wildlife, and appreciate the views from inside - looking up at the massive crater walls and appreciating the sheer size of the formation from within. There are also a variety of interesting sites inside the makhtesh, such as Ha-Minsara ("The Saw-Mill"). This sandstone hill is a rare phenomenon and stunning geological formation. On top of the hill are blocks of exposed stone, formed in such a way as to resemble symmetrical pillars placed in a heap, like boards in a mill or carpenter's shop. This is just some of the natural beauty awaiting you inside the crater.

Zin Valley

One of the biggest rivers in Israel formed the breathtaking and massive Zin Valley, alight with the beauty of nature. This vast oasis in the middle of the Negev offers a chance to appreciate the stunning contrast between the lush foliage of the valley and the stark desert just beyond. This area has been hospitable for thousands of years (while modern technology was needed to make much of the surrounding area habitable) beginning in the Nabatean Period. Take in the beauty of Ein Avdat National Park, which offers amazing views and storied hiking trails. Spend an hour or so following trails with your guide and arriving at some great panoramas for family photo taking. You even have a chance to dip into the refreshing springs of the Zin Valley, where a waterfall in the middle of the desert will inspire awe and provide an opportunity for relaxation and reflection.

Authentic Bedouin Camp

An Arab ethnocultural group, the Bedouins are a proud and noble people who have long inhabited the Arabian and Syrian deserts, among others. Blazing a trail and living where few others could, the Bedouins have long been a nomadic people, and facilitated trade between disparate communities across Israel and the surrounding area before the growth of modern infrastructure. A real Bedouin camp is something to be seen, with all the comforts of their homes ready to be packed up and moved at a moment's notice. Their rich culture includes a strong tradition of song and dance, as well as art, coupled with the bounty of a rich trade with surrounding communities.

PLEASE NOTE: For an additional fee, rather than simply driving by the camp, you can arrange to go in and have tea or a meal, as part of a local ritual and get up close and personal with a slice of Bedouin life.

These activities represent a full day's trip and a great cross section of the Negev area and local life. However, if you have different interests, consult with Ramon Desert Tours to find an itinerary that more closely matches your family's interests. They are there to work with you.

Interested in booking this (or a similar) desert tour? Contact them (and mention RealFamilyTrips.com for some consideration):

Website: www.ramontours.com/201041/English
Reference: Oded
Office Phone: 972-52-3962715
Email: odedbaba@gmail.com

Back to the Big City - Drive back to Jerusalem

To situate yourself for a final day, with a little more touring, and your eventual trip home, it is time to head back to Jerusalem. Once again taking route 40, you'll enjoy a similar scenic drive back. If you stick the the suggested timetable, finishing your Mitzpe Ramon tour around 5 PM, you'll have the added benefit of enjoying the sunset over the Negev during your drive back. This stunning vista will be a memorable end to your day and place a nice cap on your time in this area of natural beauty.

Logistics - Day 11

Suggested Order of Stops:

1. Full Day (8 hour) tour with Ramon Desert Tours, Including Zin Valley, Ramon Crater and a Bedouin Camp
2. 2-3 Hour Drive back to Jerusalem

Things to Bring/Note:

- Looser clothing for a warm day of exploring
- Bathing suits in case you take a dip in the spring, and a change of clothes for after
- Comfortable, waterproof shoes for walking and possibly entering the springs. We recommend Keen water shoes for comfort and reliability
- We recommend having a rental car for the day
- Plenty of bottled water for the day

Day 12 - Jerusalem, Wrapping Up and Heading Home

They say the sign of a good vacation is that you don't want it to be over, and we hope that at this point in your journey, this is true for you and your family. Nevertheless, all good things come to an end and after one last day of fun, learning and family togetherness, it is time to head back.

Use this time to listen to your children, see if there is anything they feel they have missed, and not push them too hard if they are beginning to grow tired. While there may be a strong desire to get in a few last things, it isn't worth spoiling great memories already made with a difficult final day. Alternately, if everyone is aching for more of Israel before departing, then it isn't the time to slack off. Listen to each other and make sure everyone is on the same page.

We hope this chance to explore Israel together has also afforded you some time to get to know one another better, and to grow both as individuals and as a family. One more day in the great city of Jerusalem will have you taking in sites and picking up last minute gifts and souvenirs before going "wheels up" on your return flight home.

A pair of museums will help round out your educational experience in Israel during this last day in Jerusalem. Some flex time has also been built in for shopping, or any other last minute pursuits you want to get in. Make as much or as little of this last day as your family desires, and enjoy a safe trip home.

Experience Israel Through the Story of One of its Greatest Sons- Tour the Begin Museum and Heritage Center

Menachem Begin was an Israeli politician and statesman, who served as the nation's sixth prime minister between the years of 1977 and 1983. He was co recipient of the Nobel Peace prize in 1978, along with then Egyptian President Anwar Sadat. He also founded the Likud party of Israeli politics, which currently (as of summer 2015) holds power in the Knesset and the office of prime minister.

One of the most pivotal and recognizable figures in Israeli government and politics, Begin was born in Poland and lived through the time of the Holocaust, working on the underground on through the establishment of the state of Israel. His is a story of tragedy as well as triumph, as he helped build the nation and then find a place for it in the world. His involvement with conflict in Lebanon in 1982 was polarizing, yet lends another element to his story that mirrors that of the larger Israeli experience. From struggling to survive to learning how to work with the world, both Begin and Israel suffered through growing pains to achieve greatness.

The experience at the Begin museum is a powerful one, as this experimental, multimedia experience seeks to tell the story of both the man, and the nation he helped to prosper. You and your family will embark on a journey through history that features historical re enactments and reconstructions, rare documentary footage, interactive exhibits that utilize modern technology - all tied together through surround sound narration. The idea is to walk you through the history rather than simply reading it, to both experience and "participate" in Begin's life as you learn about the man and the nation of Israel.

The experience will also be a powerful one for your family, as you tie together knowledge you have gained throughout your trip. A member of Irgun and the Jewish underground, the story of Begin will bring back elements of history you explored in the Museum of Underground Prisoners days earlier. Similarly, Begin's father and his fascination with Herzl, and the influence both of these men had on the late prime minister will be aided by your newfound knowledge of the founder of Zionism.

This retelling of the Israeli story, through the eyes of one of its great leaders, will be aided by the context and knowledge of your entire trip. Allow the power of history to add to this experience, as well as to reinforce the education you and your children have received. This perfect last day stop is not one to be missed.

Phone: +972 2-565-2020

Address: 6 Sh.A.Nakhon St. , Jerusalem

Email: info@begincenter.org.il

Website: http://begincenter.org.il/en/

Hours: Sunday - Monday and Wednesday - Thursday, 9 AM - 4:30 PM. Tuesday 9 AM - 7 PM. Friday 9 AM - 12:30 PM. Closed Saturdays.

Approximate Length: 1 1/2 Hours

Approximate Cost: $7 Adults, $5 Children. Family rates available

A Tribute to Heroes- Visit the Memorial at Ammunition Hill

In what is currently the Ma'alot Dafna neighborhood, stands a relic of Israel's past and a tribute to its heroes. The site was built in the 1930's as an officer's training center by the British during the period of Mandate, with a large ammunition stockpile in the hill lending the site its name. During the War of Independence in 1948, the site was conquered by Jordan, along with other parts of Jerusalem. For 19 years, the city was divided in two, with Israel and Jordan each claiming half of the Jerusalem we all know today.

During the 6 Day War of 1967, the site constituted a key battleground, one which Israeli paratroopers broke through to retake the Old CIty of Jerusalem and recapture the lands surrounding Ammunition Hill for Israel. After a decisive victory, not without loss, Israel stood at the dawning of a new age. The brave soldiers who fought so valiantly at this site offered hope to the nation.

During the rebuilding that was to follow the 1967 war, plans were made to develop the area in order to further cement an Israeli presence. Military commanders and the families of fallen soldiers appealed to preserve the battle site at Ammunition Hill as a memorial to the 182 soldiers who gave their lives there. Their wish was granted, and today the hill and the memorial stand as a tribute to the soldiers, the time in history, and the developing nation.

When you visit today there is much to see and to do. The "Wall of Honor" is a tribute to the heroism and courage of Jewish soldiers who have fought in defense of their homeland. You will also find a memorial site for the 66th Paratroopers Brigade, who recaptured the site during the Six Day War. Also preserved are the original trenches and bunkers, as well as an observation point from which you can look out over all of Israel.

The site has a museum with exhibits and a movie about the battle for Jerusalem, offered in six languages (Hebrew, English, Spanish, French, Portuguese and Russian). There is also an interactive light show, which serves as another presentation about the war, and includes a scale model of Jerusalem on the eve of the Six Day War.

This powerful location offers a chance for reflection and pays homage to the brave men and women who made your entire vacation possible. Tie off your journey through this amazing land by paying respects to those who fought, and those who died, to build a free nation in which so many people can work, live, and grow together.

Phone: +972-2-582-9393

Address: 5 Zalman Shragai St. Jerusalem, 91181

Emai: info@g-h.org.il

Website: www.g-h.org.il/en/

Hours: Sunday - Thursday, 9:00 AM - 5:00 PM. Friday, 9:00 AM - 1:00 PM.

Approximate Cost: Admission is free, donations are welcome.

Last Minute Activities - Shop, Tour or Anything Else You Need

While everyone's itinerary, departure time, and other nitty-gritty details will vary - it is important to build in some flex time. It may be a last minute trip to pick up orders for gifts you might have placed, or to buy the souvenirs you weren't sure about and thought you might go back for. It may be a quick meal to fill you up for the trip, or a shopping spree for last minute keepsakes and gifts to bring home.

Besides the fact that you need to allow some time as a contingency against the unexpected, it is always nice to have a little padding at the end of a long trip in case anyone feels they may have missed something. Did you never get around to trying that ice cream shop that the kids have been begging you to go to? Never found something for a cousin's upcoming birthday? Fill in your last minute needs *and* last minute wants. Check in with the kids, see what is on everyone's list and accomplish as much as you can. You can always sleep on the plane!

Logistics - Day 12

Suggested Order of Stops:

1. Guided Tour at the Begin Museum
2. Visit to Ammunition Hill with possible activities
3. Last minute shopping, dining, wandering or anything else - "play it by ear"
4. Travel to airport and home

Things to Bring/Note:

- Layered clothing for city exploring and later, flight
- Be sure to double check room to not leave anything behind
- Double check outlets to make sure you haven't left chargers plugged in and forgotten
- Pack reading material, small games, and other entertainment to keep children happy during the return trip
- Fully charge devices for the flight back
- Be sure to download music, movies, ebooks and other digital materials before boarding

Part VI of the accompanying children's stories goes with today's itinerary and can be found on page 106. We recommend reading the story the night before, or morning of today's journey. Following this last part of the story is an epilogue to enjoy as a family.

Our Hope for You

Throughout this book we have endeavored to provide the best in background information, quality activities and excursions, as well as connections to quality providers within the nation of Israel.

From great museums to scenic hikes, extreme adventures to cultural experiences - we hope we have been able to provide a well-rounded look at a country with so much to offer families.

While 12 days is barely enough time to scratch the surface on a visit to Israel, what we have put together has hopefully been able to give you and your children an overview of different peoples and areas, as well as a background on the country - from its roots to its inception, and on into its present day.

As family vacation is as much about the company as it is the destination, we hope that seeing these sights and experiencing these journeys together as a family will provide you with incredible opportunities for bonding, for growth, and for getting to know each other as you get to know this storied land.

Now may be the time to venture home, but it should not be an end to the experience. We hope you took lots of pictures, which you will all enjoy sharing with one another, as well as friends and extended family. It is a great way to relive vacation memories and hold on to the experiences for years to come. We also recommend following up your trip with family discussions. Talk about the things you said and did while away. Keep an eye on the news and share about developments that may interest your children, as they have a new investment in a people and land they may not have known about before.

Whether it was sharing in the thrill of a rock climbing experience, marveling together at a beautiful sunset, loving the same plate of hummus or Jerusalem mixed grill, or crying together at a memorial - hold dear the feelings that made the trip special and do your best to relive them after your return. That same closeness, that same emotion can be yours at home, as you and your children have experienced something together that no one can ever take away.

Children's Story: An Amazing Adventure in Time and Space

To help augment the experience of children travelling to Israel and families using this book as a guide, we have included this fun tale of adventure and intrigue as three young children travel through time on their family trip to Israel.

A work of historical fiction, meant to be enjoyed by children, young adults, and the family as a whole - this story will help lend context and an element of excitement to your trip. Read it before you go to build up anticipation, or on evenings during the trip as a bedtime story to tease the next day's activities or reflect on what you just saw.

Keeping children engaged, and offering something for every member of the family on their own level, is an important part of our mission. This fun and educational "book within a book" is aimed to help accomplish that.

The story is broken into seven parts, and takes place at locations actually included in the main itinerary. While it can be read all in one shot, we have broken it up to allow the events of the story to unfold alongside your vacation. At various points throughout the 12 day trip we have included references to come here, labeled Story Part I, Part II, etc. We encourage you to read it as a serial piece in this manner, letting the events of the main characters fuel your own children's senses of wonder, imagination and excitement as they explore Israel.

We hope you and your children enjoy this opportunity to let history "come alive" and encourage you to learn as you go. You may also want to allow children to read it themselves, and serve as "teachers" for the rest of the family as you go on your trip. The possibilities for fun are endless. Enjoy!

Part I

Sophia is a precocious 12 year old. Her brother Avery, age 9, has a heart of gold and a curious streak. Along with their adorable 4 year old sister Vera, the trio is enjoying their family vacation to Israel, while still on the hunt for some adventure of their own.

The siblings are currently in Hezekiah's Tunnels, far beneath the commotion of people exploring the ancient City of King David. They like the fact that no one above knows what they are up to, as if they are on a secret mission walking through the dark, wet tunnel, and splashing in the chilly water.

As Avery splashes his sisters yet *again*, Sophia turns and Vera squeals. However, before either sister can complain about the water, all three realize that their fun has caused them to lag behind the group. Their parents and older siblings have long since pressed forward in the cave, and their guide is nowhere to be seen.

Alone and in the dark, Sophia begins to worry, but Avery and Vera are still having nothing but fun. Avery reaches up to touch a mark on the wall, one the guide had told them was made over 2,000 years ago by pick axes used in the digging of the tunnel.

His finger gets stuck.

He calls out to Sophia, who is growing tired of her brother's horseplay. She says that it is time to find their parents and put an end to this.

"I'm going on ahead to find everyone," she exclaims as she picks up Vera to carry her ahead.

"But I don't want to be alone in this tunnel!" he replies, his voice starting to tremble a little.

"You have your headlamp, it's not *that* dark, I'll only be a minute, you are going to be fine."

"Just pull my arm, I'm only a little stuck. Just help me out and I swear we'll go right back to mom and dad."

Sophia sighs and sets Vera down to splash around some more in the water, as she starts to try to pull her little brother free. As they push and pull, shake and sway, gasp and strain, suddenly, something happens.

The pair hear a faint click and Avery feels something near his hand move. The gash in the wall starts to tremble and quake until all of the sudden, the tunnel opens up.

Sophia and Avery just stand there in awe. A whole new tunnel had appeared, right before their eyes! They stand and stare at each other in disbelief.

Vera wanders over and asks, "What's this!?"

Startled, Sophia is the first to reply:

"Wow! Was that there a second ago? That can't be real. I think our eyes are playing tricks on us. Ok, we really should…"

"Yes, we *should*…" Avery added.

"Yes," continued Sophia, "Should, should definitely meet back up with the group."

"Of course, that's the right thing to do. But still…"

"Of course, we could just…take a peek, right?" Sophia said, finishing the thought they both shared.

"Yay!!!" exclaims Vera, cementing the group's decision to press on.

Knowing that they needed to find their family, and frankly a little shocked and maybe even a little scared, the mischievous streak in the siblings wins out as they decide to press on into the cave.

"We'll just take a quick look," Avery said, in an answer to a question none of them asked.

Over the initial fear, all of their minds were buzzing with excitement. Would they find treasure? Ancient history? Maybe they would get a museum named after them!

Avery and Sophia each grab one of Vera's hands as they gingerly step into the new tunnel, the opening closes behind them and they are now trapped.

So much for just taking a little peek.

While the tunnel is dark, they have their headlamps, and they can see that it isn't so different from the passage they were just in. They are scared but not terrified, and growing bolder by the minute. Since Sophia and Avery are both adventurous, and they realize their screams won't be heard in these massive tunnels, they decide to follow this new tunnel to see where it leads.

A few minutes later they end up outside in the bright sunlight and they see a bunch of men dressed in ancient looking clothes, hauling massive loads of dirt up from a hole. Up and down the men go, and at the same time they are clanging as if to signal something to someone else somewhere. This is surely a strange sight, but then again they have seen some things happen in Jerusalem that they would never see at home.

The men don't see Avery, Sophia or Vera, but soon a group of young kids emerges, seemingly out of nowhere, and surrounds them. The kids are also wearing clothes from what seems to be ancient times.

One of the older of the boys, about 9 or 10 years old, comes over and addresses Avery in what Avery understands to be Hebrew.

He says, "Shalom!"

Avery, thinking that is the boy's name, says "Hi Shalom, I am Avery."

Shalom grins and says, in Hebrew again, "Shalom, Ani Avi" (hello, my name is Avi).

Avery realizes his mistake and laughs. Then, in very elementary Hebrew he introduces himself and his sisters. In a mixture of broken Hebrew, English and lots of hand gestures, it becomes quickly apparent to Avery and Sophia that they have traveled back in time some 2,000 years to the time the tunnels were built.

Avi explains the story behind the tunnel, that the brave and noble King Hezekiah had come up with the idea to build the tunnel because the city was about to be attacked. The Assyrian army would cut off the city from its water supply, but clever King Hezekiah figured out that if they dug an underground channel to the water, the Assyrians wouldn't know, and even if they did, couldn't block it!

Avi explains to the siblings exactly what is going on in the tunnels. He says that the noises are nothing to be afraid of, and that men started digging on both sides of the tunnel and intend to meet in the middle. The clanging sounds they hear let one team know where the other is, so they stay on track and have an idea of how close they are to their brothers on the other side.

Men have been working day and night, Avi continued, to complete the tunnels because the approaching army could arrive at any time, and the fate of the southern kingdom of Israel depends on the project to keep them safe. The Assyrians mean to exile them, or worse, and so men work around the clock, in tight spaces, with only candles to light their way as they clear out debris behind them. They know that if they don't finish in time, they could be doomed.

The children descend back into the tunnel. Just then, a *very* loud noise rings throughout the area.

"Was that one of those sounds that let you know where the other workers are?" Avery asks, hoping he is right.

Then more sounds, rhythmic and increasing in volume, start to echo all around them.

"I'm not so sure!" exclaims Avi,"those sound like hoofs."

Scared of what approaching horses might mean, Avi ushers the siblings down another passage towards safety. He shows them a rocky crevice in the cave wall and tells them to all push inside. Before Sophia, the last to enter, can follow her brother and sister, Avi reaches out for her hand. He pushes a small piece of silver into it and asks her to keep it safe.

As the three of them push into the crevice, it takes a minute for their eyes to adjust to the new light. Sophia turns back to thank Avi but realizes he has disappeared. Now able to see in the tunnel, the siblings realize that something has changed, something is different, and none can say exactly what is happening to them…

Part II

Sophia, Avery and Vera push deeper into the crevice they were left in, as the loud noises seem to have died down. As the trio gently edges along a passage barely wide enough for them to all squeeze through, they realize that very suddenly, everything had stopped.

It was dead quiet.

There was no sound, no light and the air had taken on a thicker, mustier feel. It felt warmer and more humid, almost like a totally different place.

"What do we do now?" Sophia asked, her genuine lack of direction showing through in her words.

"I'm not sure" Avery added, somehow glad to hear the encroaching fear in his big sister's voice, assuring him he was not alone in feeling scared of the whole situation.

Only young Vera seemed to have a handle on things, having pushed past her siblings to lead the charge forward. It was all still a game to her, and she was curious to see what was going to happen next.

Holding hands for safety, the three siblings formed a chain, with Vera at the lead, Avery in the middle, and Sophia bringing up the rear. The sisters used their free hands to feel along the walls of the cave, or was it a tunnel? Who knew anymore? All they could say for certain was that they needed to press forward.

Then, they heard a sound.

It was soft at first, like a scraping, or maybe a chirping. Something low and not quite rhythmic, but regular enough to catch their attention. Sophia thought it might be rats, or mice, or something else she wanted nothing to do with. Coincidentally, Avery *also* had the thought that it could be a mouse, and how much fun it would be to see that his sister wanted nothing to do with that. To curious Vera it was just something to investigate and move towards, her siblings scrambling to catch up.

As they pressed on, the sound got louder until, at last, a faint light broke up ahead of them. It was dim and far away, but they closed the distance quickly. The light came from the ceiling of the now widening tunnel, and as they got closer they could make out the outline of a small hole. The scraping sound got louder as well until finally, the trio arrived just under the mouth of the opening. Suddenly, a cloud of dirt and debris came down through the hole, kicking up dust and causing the young family members to cough.

Just as they were wiping the dirt from their eyes and trying once again to get their bearing, something happened.

From the hole in the ceiling, clearly visible from the light above, popped an upside down human head.

"Shalom?" said the head, wearing a thick beard and a curious expression.

Sophia and Avery grasped each other's hands tightly. Too tightly. Painfully tightly, as they turned to each other to scream. But before they could, Vera chimed in.

"Shalom!" said the four year old, with genuine enthusiasm. She then continued forward.

Mustering the kind of courage only made possible by a need to protect their sister, Avery and Sophia followed until they were directly under the hole and stood up, to see that they were just under a small room. The strange head, or rather, the entire man whose head had strangely poked down into the hole was inside, and one by one they pulled themselves up into the room.

The musty smell was even stronger here than it had been in the tunnels, and "musty" was a generous word to use. It was smelly. Not like trash or anything gross, but like sweat. It smelled like the gym locker room at the community center back home after a basketball game. As they looked around, they saw that it wasn't much of a room at all. Barely bigger than a closet, and one whole wall was just iron bars.

Was this a jail cell?!

As the siblings struggled to get their bearings, their eyes fell on the disheveled man who had poked his head down into the hole. As they struggled for words, once again it was Vera who broke the silence.

"My name is Vera, what's yours?"

Sophia stood shocked and Avery was too at first, then saw his chance to shine. After hearing "Shalom" come from the man just a second before, Avery stood tall and straightened out his back, ready to once again begin practicing his very best entry-level Hebrew.

"My name is Shmuel young Vera, but all my friends call me Shmu. That is what you should call me."

They stood once more in disbelief, as Avery quickly deflated upon realizing that he would not be able to save the day as the family Hebrew translator this time.

"Welcome to my home" Shmu added, with a wry grin on his face.

Sophia, Avery and Vera were all surprised by how articulately and eloquently Shmu spoke, for someone who looked the way he did and was rolling around on the floor, climbing out of holes. Then again, their parents had always told them not to judge a book by its cover.

Remembering many other things her parents had told her, Sophia quickly snapped to attention and stepped in front of her siblings, big sister instincts in full effect.

"Are we in jail right now? Are you a prisoner here?" asked Sophia, not accusingly but still concerned.

"You are observant children" replied Shmu, "and I'm not sure whether I am more amazed at how observant you are or that there are children here. Yes, I am a prisoner, but I am a prisoner in my own home, I am in Jerusalem on a land that will soon be free, just as I will."

"Wait! A prisoner? What did you do?" Avery asked, quick to get to the point. Sophia gave her brother a loving smack on the back, as if to indicate that it was a rude question, but none of them had ever met a prisoner. Are you allowed to ask that?

"Do not worry young ones" Schmu began, "I am not a bad person who did bad things. I am in this jail for my beliefs, for my politics, and for fighting to free Israel."

The three siblings let out a sigh of relief, as they grew more curious.

"I am from the Irgun," Shmu continued. "The National Military Organization in the Land of Israel. My friends and I fight against the British occupation and dream of a free and Independent Israel."

Shmu pointed to a carving on the wall, which he explained was the symbol of the Irgun. A hand grasping a rifle over a crude outline of Israel. He explained that he made this carving himself, to make it feel like home even though he was in jail.

"And is that why you speak English so well?" Avery asked, referring to the British presence in Jerusalem.

"I have learned a great many things from them, and hope they have from me, though I want nothing more than for the land to be a free and safe place for my children to live."

"But Israel is a free and Independent nation" Sophia exclaims.

"Ah, this innocence and imagination of children" Shmu remarks. "You inspire us all, and I hope that because of your belief, one day it will be so. War is coming, I am sad to say."

Shmu explains to the children that he never hurt anyone, but is rather, a political prisoner. He was forced to make coffins for British soldiers and police officers, told that he would have to help those he had disagreed with on the outside. He sees the growing tensions around the city of Jerusalem and the land of Israel, and believes a great war for independence is on its way. He wants nothing more than to be part of the efforts, to help serve and to see his dreams become reality. He lived in this cell with several other men, but he was the leader. He was supervisor of all the men in his cell and was the only one with his own bed.

"Where are your friends now?" Vera asked.

"Funny you should mention it, because tonight is our night!" Shmu exclaimed, clearly excited about the prospect.

Shmu goes on to say that they have been working on a great plan for many months. This cell is on the outside wall of the prison, near the fence. They had been digging under the bed for a long time, out towards the street. Their tunnel connects to a sewer pipe and under the fence to the outside world. Some of their friends on the outside had worked on the other end, posing as sewer workers, and were right now pretending to fix the pipe.

"It is easier to show you than to tell you!" exclaims Shmu as he jumps back into the tunnel, awfully ecstatic for someone about to walk through the sewers.

Once again rushing to keep up with Vera, Avery and Sophia follow their young sister and new friend through the tunnel, into a pipe and along the ground towards freedom. As they reach the end the fresh air hits them like a wall. The light explodes over their faces and they are so happy to once again feel a cool breeze and a warm sun on their faces after so much time underground. They push their way through and out of the hole, looking around for Shmu.

He was nowhere to be found.

As their eyes once again adjusted, the siblings looked around to get their bearings. Vera stooped down to pick up an interesting piece of silver off the ground, and all of them tried to figure out where they were, and what would happen next…

Part III

Back above ground for the first time in what seemed like hours, Avery, Sophia and Vera were all happy to stretch their legs, but worried about where they might be. Excitement quickly outweighed the worry as the sun warmed them up and the three siblings had a chance to breathe easier.

All this adventure was something they might just get used to.

The three of them looked around and saw strange, yet somehow familiar, sights. Along the ridge were a line of trees with beautiful, waxy leaves that glistened in the sun. There were several small buildings to one side, all very similar to each other, like low slung bungalows that seemed to blend right into the countryside. There was a large barn and what looked like a schoolhouse. It was beautiful and rustic, with tractors and plows dotting a landscape of clotheslines and campsites.

"I think I know where we are!" Avery exclaimed, "This looks like a kibbutz."

The children had been to one of the collective farming communities years earlier and recognized the setup. Sophia had a point however.

"You're right, it does look like a kibbutz, but shouldn't we be in Jerusalem, right outside a prison? It looks like we're in the middle of nowhere!"

She was right, and they all knew it. Luckily Avery, always ready to break the silence had one other point to make.

"Well if it is a kibbutz," Avery started, "then they must have some food, and something smells pretty good to me. I'm starving."

Sophia rolled her eyes and Vera followed suit. The sisters both wondered how he could think of food at a time like this.

At this point, more important than any amount of delicious Jerusalem mixed grill, the siblings realized they were not alone.

They heard footsteps ahead, and voices talking faintly over the ridge. They wondered if they should run towards them or away, was it safe or dangerous? They had sure met some interesting people lately, but they had no business running up to strangers. At the same time, they had no idea where their parents and older siblings were or, for that matter, where *they* were!

Then their decision was made for them.

A young girl ran up behind them and tapped Sophia on the shoulder. Sophia jumped just a little and the girl giggled. Then Vera giggled. Suddenly, aware of how funny it was, they all started giggling.

"Hello my funny new friends" she started, "my name is Rachel. Who are you?"

"I am Avery" the brother offerd, enjoying his assumed role as emissary of the family, "and these are my sisters Sophia and Vera."

"Very nice to meet you all" Rachel continued, "are you new here?"

"I guess you could say that" replied Sophia, "though we aren't really sure where 'here' is"

"Welcome to Kibbutz Tzova" said Rachel, "let me show you around, it is very exciting to have new friends!"

The three siblings followed Rachel, who they found out was 10 years old, right in between Avery and Sophia. Vera darted alongside the group, always managing to be either just ahead of or just behind everyone else, her boundless energy kept her moving faster than most.

As they got over the first ridge they saw the source of the footsteps and mumblings of earlier, it was a group of men and women on patrol, guns slung over their shoulders. In fact, the more they walked around, the more military gear they saw, and at one point they could even see a firing range off in the distance, with people lining up to practice shooting at targets. Rachel assured them not to be afraid, there was no danger here and no fighting going on, just training.

She said that they were Palmach, soldiers ready to fight for Israeli independence. Both the men and the women here were trained soldiers who took their duty very seriously. They trained here on the kibbutz, but also worked the land and the children like her went to school. They shared everything and worked together. They protect the budding nation of Israel so that its people can be free and safe.

While Sophia wondered to herself why everyone seemed to think that Israel wasn't free yet, and just *when* it was right now, Avery's mischievous streak was shining through. Spotting a big bale of hay, rolled up like a giant donut, he decided to climb up to the top, to show off for his sisters and new friend. He quickly made it to the top and began jumping for joy, showing how impressive his climb was.

The only trouble being that, like a donut, the bale had a big hole in the middle.

Suddenly, Avery landed from one of his leaps into the air, but sank a bit further than he was planning on, his legs lodging themselves in the hole. Just his arms and head stook out, flailing around as Avery suddenly looked like a giant snowman, or maybe more like a marshmallow with a boy sticking out of it.

Everyone found themselves giggling once again.

Rachel and Sophia turned the bale on its side, and each grabbed one of Avery's arms to pull him out. It took some effort, but soon he was free, and quite red in the face as his big show off hadn't quite gone as planned.

They all look around for Vera, but couldn't find her.

The three begin calling out, and quickly spot her just up ahead on the trail. Suddenly, a gunshot rang out. Vera cried. Rachel rushed to her side and pointed at the now not so far off shooting range. She said that they are just practicing, and there is nothing to be afraid of.

Avery and Sophia rushed to comfort their sister, who is obviously afraid of this loud new development. Recognizing that her new friends aren't kibbutzniks like her, and might need some time to get used to how things are done, Rachel had an idea.

"Follow me" Rachel says, "I know something that will make us all feel better."

Avery, Sophia and a much calmer Vera, wrapped up in her sister's arms, began a long walk across the kibbutz, towards the rapidly setting sun. As the air cooled off and night set in, so did the tensions of the day, and the four children eventually arrived at a campground, surrounded by the people of the kibbutz.

The children settled in with all of the kibbutzniks and Rachel told them about "Kumzitz." This was the nightly campfire, the "come sit" period where everyone washed away all the worries of the day by sitting, together, around the fire.

The children saw a great feast being prepared, with fresh vegetables and delicious meats being heated on the fire. Some of the men had guitars and were starting to play slow, melodic songs. Children ran and danced around, and it felt like some sort of wonderful party.

Rachel explained that while they all work very hard, both at their training and their farming, they also love nothing more than to just enjoy each other's' company. Hiking is a favorite activity, which the siblings can identify with, having gone on so many great hikes with the rest of their family, all over the world.

As everyone ate, in between songs, some of the older men burst in with stories. Some are old folk tales, that teach lessons and remember history. Others are personal stories, and Rachel says her Uncle Yaakov is famous for them.

Yaakov is a big man, with a very full beard and broad shoulders, yet still somehow wiry and thin. When he dances he looks like a strong breeze might topple him over, yet no matter how much he bends, he always snaps back up. He reminds the children of one of those inflatable toys that can't be knocked over.

Yaakov began telling a story of a great hike he once took as a boy, very young, around the age of "that one" he said, pointing to Avery, who smiled. Yaakov said he had packed up everything he owned for a very long hike, in one large bag, as big as himself, maybe bigger, that he had slung over his back. He hiked up and down the hills, under the hot sun, with no water, for 500 kilometers. When he was hungry, he took snakes with his bare hands and cooked them over a fire he started with only two rocks. On and on the story went, for what seemed like hours, painting a questionable picture of heroism.

"I don't think you really could have done all those things!" exclaimed Avery, smelling a fib when he heard one.

Rachel leaned over and whispered to him that this was chizbat, tall tales, and her Uncle Yaakov was famous for his long stories, mixing fact and fiction.

A long laugh came out from the group around the campfire. "You've been called out!" said one man, "the boy is onto you Yaakov."

"The real problem isn't that your stories aren't true" said another, "it's that they only have one character...you."

"The problem isn't that my stories only have one character" offered Yaakov, "it's that I myself have no character!"

Everyone laughed again, even harder than before. As the fire roared and the people once again broke out in song, the three siblings grew tired from another long day. Sophia looked over at Avery, already asleep with a big smile on his face. Vera had long since lost her energy for the day and was curled up at her sister's side. Yaakov walked alongside the trio, offering a pat on the head to young Avery for being a good sport. He tucked a small piece of silver into his sleeping hand and walked off. Barely recognizing this, Sophia allowed herself to drift off into the night, dreamily wondering what adventure would come next.

Part *IV*

Soundly asleep and sprawled out on each other for comfort and warmth, the three siblings were content in their quiet slumber. Unfortunately, this wouldn't last for long.

"Hee-Haaaaaw!" came the sound, loud and percussive. Shaking the three children from their slumber.

It was a donkey.

Sophia, Avery and Vera's eyes all shot open very quickly, the startled siblings barely knowing what was happening. They jumped to their feet just in time, as a large cart pulled by the donkey nearly runs them over!

Startled and disoriented, the three children held each other tight as they slowly edged back from the cart. They marveled at the large, wooden box, draped in fancy cloth with gold inlay, over large wooden wheels that clattered against cobblestone underfoot. The donkey let out another loud bray and sneezed, which if you have ever seen a donkey sneeze, is not a gentle thing to behold.

The sun was once again hot and bright overhead, the night seems to have long since passed. As the trio quickly shook off their slumber and adjusted their eyes, they realized that they were once again far from where they started.

Avery, Vera and Sophia now stand in a city square. All around them are wooden shacks and stands, more carts, and what must be hundreds of people. Stone towers rise up around them, and everyone seems to be running about, busy and set to their tasks.

"Wow!" Vera offers, uttering the simple word that best sums up what they are all thinking at that moment.

Wow indeed. The three siblings continue to take in the scene, and there is simply nothing else that can describe it. Among those milling about the plaza are knights in full plate mail, with crisp white tunics overlaid with red crosses that cover their scaly metal adornments. There are men and women in the brightest robes they have ever seen, rich purples and deep oranges, flowing and beautiful garments that cover them head to toe. There are turbaned men and veiled women, mixed among those barely clothed, with simple rags covering them as they shuffle among those more impressively dressed. The shaved heads of monks in simple brown robes glisten in the sun as they pass by the three children, too focused to notice them.

In one direction it looks like the movie "Aladdin" come to life, and just feet from that, a scene right out of a King Arthur book. They hear people talking, yelling and carrying on in more languages than they can count. There is Hebrew for sure, as well as what the older children know to be Arabic. The monks chant in what must be Latin, while others cry out in tongues none of the children have ever heard before.

"It's like we're in Times Square" Sophia exclaims, filled with a similar feeling she has had when visiting the New York City landmark with her family.

"But without all the neon signs" Avery adds, quick to point out that something here is decidedly different.

"It smells funny" Vera chimes in, pointing out one fact that none of the siblings could deny.

It did smell funny, even funnier than any part of New York ever could. It was a mix of animals and a number of people who didn't seem to bathe as much as the siblings' parents made sure they did. At the same time there were exotic spices and cooking fires mixed in, creating a truly unique aroma that only added to the visual scene.

It was unlike anything they had ever experienced, and it was utterly confusing.

Avery and Sophia each grabbed one of Vera's hands, lest she find her way in front of another cart or one of the many horses they had seen crossing the city square. They all held each other close as they set out to explore this new and exciting environment.

They looked up and saw massive city walls, with ramparts that extended to a brick gateway looking out over the sea. To one side was a bathhouse. There were tall fortresses and walls above where they stood, as well as below the city level. They saw a small church and a beautiful synagogue, and everyone who passed them seemed like a character in some wonderful movie.

That was when it hit Sophia.

"This must be Akko!" she exclaimed, unsure if she was excited or troubled by this realization. "See, there is the Citadel, and the Turkish baths, all the things Mom and Dad read to us about!"

The three siblings looked around, taking in the scene with this new information in hand.

Sophia continued to explain what she had realized. She recalls the past stops, first in Hezekiah's Tunnels, then the Underground Prisoner Museum and the Palmach exhibit. She says that everything was in the trip their family had been planning, and ever since they got separated they still seemed to be following parts of the plan, in the right order, just not with their family!

"I think you're right!" Avery exclaimed, adding "and I'm pretty sure that this isn't the tour. I don't think all of these people are actors."

Sophia considered this for a moment and agreed. "You're right Avery, we're definitely still in the past; we seem to be going back to various times in the history of Israel."

While they might have been unsure of when and where they were exactly, one thing was clear: they needed to keep moving. Sophia led the charge, hoping that she could find someone who might be able to help. First, of course, she would have to find someone who spoke the right language!

As Sophia considered options, Avery, or more accurately, Avery and his famous stomach, had an idea of their own. Remembering something *he* had read about Akko before their trip, Avery thought about the famous sugar trade in the city and thought that if they were a thousand years in the past, he might as well find out what thousand year old candy tasted like!

As Sophia picked up her little sister and scouted the area for help, she spotted a young girl helping her father unload a cart full of linens and thought she had found a good prospect.

"Here, follow me Avery" she said, starting forward. But when she turned to look, her brother was already on his way, clear in the other direction.

Sophia darted across the bazaar, clutching Vera tight, and weaving around passersby as she tried to catch up with her brother.

Avery darted around sacks full of fragrant spices, tables covered in fish and other sea creatures, and merchants selling all manner of textiles, metals, and beautiful painted trinkets. Then, up ahead, he saw what he was after.

A short man with a solitary stand on the corner of the large bazaar had a table set up with tiny cones of white, crystallized sugar, tightly packed like sweet beacons among the bustling marketplace.

With Avery making a hard line for the ancient candy, Sophia was startled as a large flock of people darted in front of her, blocking her path. As she jumped back to get out of the way, her hand let go of Vera's for just a second. As a fight broke out in front of her, with one of the crowd seeming to claim another had stolen from him, Sophia was disoriented and blocked off from her goal.

Luckily, the crowd passed quickly, with the one man being chased off by the group. Terrified she has lost her siblings in this strange place, Sophia started running forward.

As the last of the crowd broke, Sophia was relieved to see her siblings up ahead. Reliably, Avery had continued to follow his instinct for sugar straight to the merchant with the white cones, and Vera has joined in on her brother's mission.

"Don't do that Avery! You have no idea how worried I was just then!" She exclaimed, her voice tinged with concern.

"I'm sorry, I just got so excited!" Avery said, truly sorry he had gotten so carried away with himself, but also excited to try his new treat.

Sophia looked over both her siblings, Avery with handfuls of sugary snacks, and Vera, staring back up at her holding a single piece of shiny, beautiful silver.

"What have you got there?" Sophia asked her sister, sensing the familiarity of it but not quite able to put her finger on why.

Before Vera could answer, or Avery could eat any of his questionable new treats, the man behind the sugar table cried out and pointed to the sky.

The three turned to see clouds moving in rapidly, blotting out the sun and darkening the entire area in a flash. They grabbed each other tight and wondered what was happening. Avery dropped his sugar while Vera grasped her silver and Sophia held both of her siblings tight.

That's when the rain started, and like everyone else, they ran for cover.

Part V

Surrounded by a crowd bustling for cover and under a cloudy sky, everything went dark for just a moment. By the time the three siblings could see again, things seemed to have calmed down significantly.

"Don't you ever run off like that again!" Sophia urged, "something could have happened! Did you even pay for that sugar you wanted so badly?"

"I was just about to" Avery pointed out, shekels in hand, as he turned around to make good on the sugar, even though he had dropped it.

Only when Avery turned around, the man with the sugar table was nowhere to be seen. In his place, stood a woman, with a much more elaborate stall than the one that had been there just a second ago, covered in fruits and vegetables.

Avery stood, dumbfounded, wondering what had happened during the brief moments of cloud cover.

Sophia caught on as well, looking at the woman, then back at her siblings. Clearly things had changed, yet again.

They looked around and found themselves in a bustling marketplace, yet somehow very different from the one they had been in moments before. Gone were the tall citadels and ancient peoples. There were no robed monks or knights in armor here. The clothing everyone wore was a bit more modern, though not as much so as theirs. People wore sandals or sturdy shoes, but mostly out of leather, not the rubberized sport shoes the three siblings had on.

Gone were the bright colors and outlandish robes. Everyone here was dressed more conservatively, like something out of an old picture of their grandparents.

"So where has your stomach landed us now?" she teased her brother.

Avery smiled sheepishly, knowing he had done the wrong thing wandering off, but the delicious smells in the air had him thinking of letting his tummy do the talking once again.

Reading her brother's mind, Sophia realized that she too was hungry, as she turned to figure out where they were now.

Just then, Vera stooped down to pick up a ball that was rolling towards her feet. She held it up to her big sister, who wondered where it came from.

Then all three siblings turned as another small girl approached them, running and out of breath.

"Thank you" said the girl. "That almost got away from me."

Vera gingerly handed the ball back to the girl, who in turn, threw it back to her friends that were trailing behind her.

"What's your name?" Vera asked, happy to meet another new friend.

"I am Rosa Navon" she offered, to which Sophia, Avery and Vera all chimed in with their names.

"I know this may sound strange" Sophia started, "but can you tell us where we are?"

"This is the Mahane Yehuda Market" Rosa replied, "it is named after my uncle, and my family helped start it.

Rosa explained how wonderful the market is, because people from all over the country come together and sell side by side. No one worries about where someone is from or what they believe, just what they have to offer. She says that she has friends from all over the world. They get to meet such interesting people, and you can find just about *anything* here.

"What we *really* need to find are our parents" Sophia exclaimed, her worry starting to show just a little more with each trip through time. She threw her arms up in the air.

As she did, the small piece of silver that Avi had given her back in the tunnel fell from her pocket. Avery spotted it, and pulled the piece he got from Yaakov on the kibbutz out of his pocket. Suddenly, he had an idea.

Remembering that Vera had found one in Akko as well, that every place they had stopped had held some small piece of silver, he thought that maybe there was some meaning to this, and it might help them get back to their family.

"Do you know anyone at the market who trades silver?" Avery asked.

"Yes!" exclaimed Sophia, having the same idea as her brother, "anything like this?" She added, picking up the piece that had fallen to the ground and showing it to Rosa.

"I think I know just the person" Rosa said, starting off across the market.

Avery, Sophia and Vera followed her, sticking close as they traversed the marketplace. It is a beautiful sight, somehow organized and chaotic at the same time. People dart back and forth, shouting in Hebrew, Arabic, and other languages. They yelled out what they were selling, prices, and sales pitches. People haggled over prices and all seemed quite friendly.

Rosa was right when she said you could find anything at the shuk. There were beautiful round oranges, brighter than any they had ever seen. Sophia had to push her brother by a table stacked high with giant rounds of sweet halvah. Breads and pitas piled as tall as Vera stood atop sprawling tables, still warm from the bakery. People squatted on small boxes and ate delicious foods. Others crowded around tables of beautiful jewelry and mosaic art. It was like a mall but all out in the open, like ones they had seen before but somehow older.

Stalls were laid out haphazardly, with not much to separate one from another. Because it was daytime and bright from the sun, it took a minute to realize that there was nothing run by electricity. No refrigerators to keep things cool, just buckets of ice. No gas stoves to cook food, but open fires and hot coals.

Eventually they wound their way through the market, amazed to have a chance to see it in its early days. Sophia grasped her brother tight to move past all the delicious treats, and Vera skipped along at her sister's side.

Then, Rosa stopped and turned back to her new friends.

"Is this what you were looking for?" She asked, stepping aside to reveal a table awash with sparkling silver, beautiful pieces of all shapes and sizes. There were small statues, menorahs and other religious pieces, along with simple jewelry and ornate tableware.

Rosa turned to the shopkeeper, and asked something none of the three could make out. The woman at the stall smiled a big smile and nodded, before reaching behind the table to grab something. She handed it to Rosa.

Rosa then turned to Vera, once again thanking her for returning her ball. She handed over the small, irregular piece of silver, just like the others the siblings had found or received, and said "this is for you." Vera said "thank you" and turned to her brother and sister, beaming at the beautiful trinket.

"Thank you for your help" Sophia says, "but what we really need is to ask some questions about what this means."

The silver saleswoman smiled broadly once more, awaiting the young siblings' questions.

Just then, a trumpet blared, washing over the market with its loud, piercing sound.

"What was that!?" Avery asks.

"That trumpet is the signal that it is time to prepare for Shabbos, and the market must close" Rosa answered.

"But...but...we just need to ask one quick question!" Avery pleaded, sensing their opportunity may be slipping away.

Just then the crowded market began shifting, with hundreds of people quickly breaking off in every direction, hustling home for the Sabbath.

Intent on not repeating their mistake in Akko, the siblings gathered close as people brushed by them on either side, surrounding the three of them.

Once the crowd passed the siblings turned to find Rosa and the shopkeeper once again but find they were gone, disappeared in the crowd. Before they could say anything, the bright sun caught something and washed over the trio in a blinding light that stunned them, just for a moment...but a moment was all it needed.

Part VI

Avery, Sophia and Vera were still blinded by the bright light. They rubbed their eyes, then blinked hard and fast to try to get their vision back. Once they could see again, they turned and noticed that the sun must have caught the top of a tall, white building.

More amazingly, as their eyes adjusted further, they turned to see that they were no longer in a marketplace, but a grove of olive trees - seemingly hundreds of them.

"It happened again!" Avery exclaimed, never quite getting used to the idea of traveling through time and space.

The scene was quiet and tranquil compared to the busy shuk, a sense of ease washed over the three of them as they surveyed the area. They seemed to be on a hilltop, and off in the distance they could see a city they knew to be Jerusalem. The more they looked, the more they realized that this is probably the best view of the city they had ever seen, and they stood, silently for a minute and took it all in.

"Where are we now?" Avery asked. "Where did all these trees come from, there must be a hundred of them!"

Just then, Sophia had another thought.

"I bet you there are exactly 182 olive trees here" she said, apparently confident in her assessment.

"No way" Avery said, "no one can count that quickly."

"I didn't count, I know where we are!"

The trio made their way over the hill and through the many trees; darting back and forth, following Sophia's lead.

They soon encountered something entirely new to them - trenches. Long winding ones, made of stones piled high to create vast and durable fortifications. Off to one side was a tank, the siblings instinctively covered their heads but soon realized it wasn't moving. The sight of these elements of war had them scared for a second, that they might have been transported to some active battlefield from Israel's past. However, the more they looked, the more they began to notice signs and plaques on everything, and that there were no soldiers to be seen.

"Ok, I give up, just where are we exactly?" Avery asked, willing to concede he didn't figure out what his big sister apparently had.

"Ammunition Hill!" exclaimed Sophia, "from the itinerary. It's on our last day, so we need to find out how to get back to our family before the trip is over!"

This added a new sense of urgency to their trek, as the thought of being left behind was not too fun. They certainly loved Israel, but they loved their family more and were ready to be back with them.

As they wove between the lines of trenches and remnants of a great battlefield, it was Avery's turn to notice something.

"Look at that, over there" Avery said, pointing to a rooftop off in the distance.

There it was, plain as day, a satellite dish pointed up to the sky. The implications of modern technology got the three even more excited.

"That means we can't possibly be in the 8th, 18th or even 19th century anymore! I think we made it back!"

Then, off in the distance, they heard a voice.

Though it was muffled by the sandbags lining the area, and the tall trench walls, the voice was the most exciting thing the trio had heard. The promise of being back in their own time, back on track, meant they could finally, really, be home.

They made their way towards the voice, as quickly as their legs would take them. After crouching through tunnels, crowding their way through marketplaces and hiking over vast hills, their energy was suddenly returned to them.

They navigated through the trenches, winding left and right, making a race out of it and having as much fun as they have ever had. The voice was growing louder with each turn, and the promise of finding people got more and more real.

Confirming suspicions, they began to be able to make out words from the now less distant voice. They heard stories of the Six Day War, and the battle fought on Ammunition Hill to secure independence for Israel.

Avery was excited, and dashed ahead towards what *has* to be a tour group.

Young Vera pulled ahead of her siblings and rounded the next bend before either of them could. Sophia became alarmed to lose sight of her, but what she heard next relieved her concern...

"Mommy!"

As Sophia and Avery caught up, they saw Vera closing the final ground between themselves and a group of people. They looked up to see that their mother was indeed there. Next to her was their father and their older siblings. They had found their family at last!

Exhausted, they ran the final steps and all but collapsed at their family's feet.

As the tour guide told a story of the war, its heroes, and Israel's duty to honor those who made the nation possible - the three siblings let out a collective and audible sigh - as suddenly everyone turned to see the commotion.

The tour guide ignored the interruption and continued on, motioning the group to follow him to the Wall of Honor.

"Shhh! You need to be respectful of this place and the rest of the tourists here" their mother urged, otherwise unaffected by their return.

Avery and Sophia looked at each other, and then at Vera. How had no one noticed they were gone. Had it been a week, a day, a minute?

What had happened to them? How had they travelled through time, following their family but moving through the past instead of the present? What had this journey meant, why had it happened and how? More importantly, had it even been real?

With their minds spinning at a hundred miles an hour, suddenly, something stopped them dead in their tracks.

Avery and Sophia turned to look at Vera, who was tugging at their mother and pointing.

At first it seemed like nothing, just Vera being Vera, until they looked in Vera's palm - the guide had just given her a small piece of silver...

Epilogue

Having enjoyed their last day, and now happily back in the arms of their family, the three siblings sit on their hotel room floor. They are still in awe of what happened to them, and enjoy having a little secret that no one else seems to understand. Their family thinks they were with them the whole time, and would never believe that they had stood with laborers, prisoners, merchants and soldiers across thousands of years of history.

Now holding six, oddly shaped pieces of silver, they wonder about what this other mystery could be all about. Why had they been given, or found, these interesting trinkets everywhere the three of them wandered?

Avery suggests that maybe they are ancient coins or other currency, and that perhaps they are now rich!

Sophia says that it might be remnants of ancient tool, and that it might belong in a museum.

They all sit, staring at the fragments, moving them around and comparing them to each other. They scratch their heads, squint their eyes, and do everything they can do to make sense of what they might mean.

Only Vera, youngest among them, could see what they really are.

"Puzzle!" she exclaims, as she begins moving the shiny fragments around.

Sure enough she is right, as the three siblings work together to assemble the shiny objects as a team.

"There is the north, with the Golan Heights!"

"And the South, with Mitzpe Ramon!"

"Here is Gush Katif!"

As they finish their task, they realize that they are staring at their entire trip. Sitting before them, in stunning silver, is all of Israel, laid out before their eyes.

"It's beautiful!" Vera exclaims.

"We can hang this in our house and never forget the most amazing vacation ever!" Avery adds.

"As if that was ever going to be a problem" Sophia said, shaking thousand year old dirt out of her shoes.

Just another day in the lives of three time traveling siblings.

The End

Appendix A: Alternate Activities

Many spend their whole lives in Israel and never experience everything it has to offer. To think it could all be done in less than two weeks would simply be unrealistic. There are so many great activities that were not included in the itineraries of this trip, not because they don't have a lot to offer - but because time, location and other logistics did not permit.

Alternately, while we have done our best to create a trip that will appeal to many families, tastes vary and priorities are different from person to person.

The following represents a cross-section of RealFamilyTrips.com's "best of the rest", in the form of activities, locations, and excursions that didn't make the cut for the main text of this book. In most cases, we will note why they were ultimately not included. In all cases we will indicate where they would best fit.

If you find anything in the main portion of this book unappealing to you, look here to "swap something out" for an option that better suits your family. If you like more or less action, here is where you can find alternate ideas to customize a trip for your family.

Also, if you plan on spending more than 12 days in Israel, you can expand upon our original itinerary by adding from this section.

Your vacation is about your family. Make sure that what you plan to do represents the best possible choices for you and your children. Appendix B has resources that can help you find even more ideas if you so need or desire.

Yad Vashem Museum, Jerusalem

Why We Omitted It: If your children are old enough and mature enough to handle this intense and powerful place, then it is a must see. Because not everyone can, we chose to leave it off the main itinerary.

Where it Goes: Jerusalem, any of days 1, 2, 7, 9 or 12

The Holocaust represents perhaps the darkest page in all of history, one marked with terrible suffering and the death of so many innocents. It also represents an important chapter in the development of Israel. It drove immigration that populated the area, increased international favor for Zionist principles, and created a sympathetic community that enabled the creation of the country. Furthermore, it has driven the attitudes, policies, and hearts of the Israeli people from day one. Through wars and invasions, terrorism and innumerable threats, the same people who survived this terror established an indomitable national spirit that will never give up and never forget.

For all these reasons and more, the Yad Vashem Museum is a must visit. While there are powerful and important museums and memorials dedicated to Holocaust studies around the world, this institute and museum in the heart of Jerusalem is particularly powerful. In Jerusalem, it is second only to the Kotel in number of annual visitors and held in high regard by locals and tourists alike.

One of the things that sets Yad Vashem apart from similar museums is the Garden of the Righteous Among the Nations. This site recognizes gentiles who, at risk to themselves and families, and without a financial or evangelistic motives, helped save Jews from genocide during the Holocaust. At the core of the mission during the founding of Yad Vashem, this exhibit and its powerful stories tell an important part of the story for both Jewish and non-Jewish visitors to appreciate and learn from.

Other exhibits here describe Jewish resistance in the Warsaw ghetto, as well as the uprisings in Sobibor and Treblinka death camps. There is a similar focus on the struggle of survivors to reach Israel. Though these retellings of pain and suffering are difficult, there is something about hearing them in

Israel, and not only knowing - but feeling - the power of this safe place which many Jews were able to finally arrive at, and the peace it has provided survivors.

This powerful site has a lot to offer your family, and even a brief visit here will provide fodder for important discussion upon returning from your trip, as you all reflect on the stories of both suffering and salvation.

Please Note: Groups of 6 or more people are required to schedule their visit in advance. Use their online Reservation Center to set up a visit. Also know that entrance to the Holocaust History Museum is not permitted for children under the age of 10. Babies in strollers or carriers will not be permitted to enter.

Address: Jerusalem, Israel - located on the western slope of Mount Herzl

Phone: +972 2-644-3802

Email: general.information@yadvashem.org.il

Website: www.yadvashem.org/yv/en/museum/#!prettyPhoto

Hours: Sunday - Wednesday, 9 AM - 5 PM. Thursday, 9 AM - 8 PM. Friday, 9 AM - 2 PM. Closed Saturdays.

Approximate Length: 1-2 Hours

Approximate Cost: FREE of charge

Ein Avdat (near Mitzpe Ramon)

Why We Omitted It: While a beautiful location in the Zin Valley, you cannot go in the water here. The views are fantastic, however our recommended guide (Oded) on day 11 knows a similar spot where you can take a Jeep ride/hike *and* be able to go in the water. When touring in August, getting the kids (and even the adults) in the water is a must!

Where it Goes: Mitzpe Ramon (Southern Israel), Days 10 or 11

Ein Avdat is an Israeli National Park, featuring water from the Avdat spring, which has cut the beautiful canyon through the Negev. Stunning features include a natural waterfall, and a pool where wild ibex come to drink and feed. This actual desert oasis is stunning in its beauty and stark in its contrast to the surrounding area.

The main trail winds through the entire park, from the lower to upper entrance, at times seemingly far out of the way due to conservation concerns. The trail is listed as easy enough for all ages as a simple walking path. However, at one point to follow the main trail, visitors are required to climb iron rungs in a rock wall. This can be avoided by taking a longer, lowland route around.

Along the way you'll see the lush greenery juxtaposed against soft chalk walls, striped with horizontal patterns. Euphrates poplars dot the trail near the En Ma'arif pools, which lie at the foot of the waterfall. The path will also walk you by caves inhabited by monks during the Byzantine period.

This beautiful and fascinating destination provides a few hours of great walking and viewing in an area that has been long admired and inhabited. If you don't plan on going into the water at the Zin Valley anyway, this may be your best best for stunning views and easy hiking.

Travel Tip: You can buy a combination day pass for this park, as well as the Avdat National Park (site of the former Nabatean city) for a discounted rate.

Address: Hwy 40, Mitspe Ramon, Israel

Phone: 08-655-5684

Email: moked@npa.org.il

Website:
www.parks.org.il/ParksAndReserves/enAvdat/Pages/default.a spx#_=_ (Hebrew)

http://old.parks.org.il/BuildaGate5/general2/company_search_ tree.php?Cat=378~All (English)

Hours: April - September, 8 AM - 5 PM. October - March, 8 AM - 4 PM.

Approximate Length: 1-2 Hours

Approximate Cost: $8 per adult, $4 per child for a day pass

Ben Gurion's Hut In Sde Boker

Why We Omitted It: Not enough time in our planned itinerary to allow for the travel required to get here. If you want to make it a priority and sacrifice some Jeep touring time or outdoor activities it could be a great option for you,

Where it Goes: Mitzpe Ramon (Southern Israel), Days 10 or 11

PLEASE NOTE: This entry is for what is commonly known as "Ben Gurion's Hut", the residence in Sde Boker. There is also a Ben Gurion House in Tel Aviv. They are similar in scope and nature, and both equally worth a visit, but in very different locations.

David Ben Gurion was Israel's first prime minister and left an indelible mark on the nation he served. It was, in part, his vision that launched the nation and set a course for its early days. Serving as defense minister in addition to prime minister, he led by an example of strength that will forever color Israel and its desire to defend its right to exist.

In addition to having a strong vision for Israel as a whole, he had a similar vision for the Negev. His desire to see a "flower bloom in the desert" led to development and made sure that this vast stretch of land would not be forsaken, but built up for Israel's future. When he retired from politics it was here, in Kibbutz Sde Boker that he and his wife Paula retreated from the public eye to go about living their vision of the Israeli dream.

The home has been left largely untouched from the days the Ben Gurions lived there, and includes family photos, books and gifts from world leaders. All informational materials are near the entrance, including information about the life, times and connection to the Negev of Mr. Ben Gurion. It is presented as an animated film, making information more accessible to children. This degree of accessibility to families is further enhanced in the yard area of the home. Here you will find three activity areas on the subject of "Ben-Gurion and the Jewish National Fund", including a sand map, two cartography maps and a matching game with ropes. In another area, "interactive tables" feature a variety of information about the man, the formation of Israel and the legacy left behind, as well as information on Sde Boker itself.

All of this comes together to present an important figure in Israeli history in a fascinating, natural setting. The interactivity makes it perfect for families, and the beautiful area and scenic drive to get here make it well worth the effort

Address: Kibbutz Sde Boker 84993

Phone: +972-(0)8-6560469

Email: Zrif.bg@gmail.com

Website: www.bgh.org.il/info/hut/hut-005.htm

Hours: Sunday - Thursday, 8:30 AM - 4 PM. Friday/Holiday Eve 8:30 AM - 2 PM. Saturday/Holiday 10 AM - 4 PM.

Approximate Length: 1 Hour

Approximate Cost: FREE of charge

Rappelling off the Tayelet

Why We Omitted It: Other rappelling adventures in other locations filled our bill. If you choose to change things up on some of the other days, or simply can't resist the views in Jerusalem, this is a great option.

Where it Goes: Jerusalem, any of days 1, 2, 7, 9 or 12

Rappelling is a great way to participate in an exciting (yet supervised) activity that will get your pulse pounding and can be scaled and adjusted to accommodate you and your children on different levels. Through or friends at Fun In Jerusalem come some great options for rappelling (or as it is sometimes known in Israel, "snappelling") in the city of Jerusalem.

This rappelling adventure is suitable **for ages 4 and up** (younger kids may rappel with a guide). The idea is to challenge each of you on your own level, for a customized experience that recognizes differences in abilities and allows you all to have a good time on your own, while still having fun together.

The Tayelet (also known as the Haas Promenade) is a perfect place to set this adventure, with sweeping views of the entire city. As you enjoy your climb, look out on landmarks like the Kotel, the Old City, the Hurva Synagogue, and the Mount of Olives - just to name a few. The location is more than just a pretty view, with a significance of its own. Mentioned in the Book of Genesis, tradition has this as the location from which Avraham first spotted Mt. Moriah.

Enjoy a famed landmark in Jerusalem combined with a fun and exciting experience, to give a new twist to a classic excursion and a truly unique view. This rappelling adventure is a great option for families who can't get enough action, as well as those who simply want to change things up.

We recommend booking through FunInJerusalem.com

Address: Hinom Valley, Jerusalem, Israel

Phone: 052-893-8921

Email: snappling@funinjerusalem.com

Website: www.challengetours.org

Approximate Length: 1-2 Hours

Approximate Cost: Varies with size of group and length of time, see www.funinjerusalem.com/rappelling/#booknow

Afrikef Monkey Park (Ben Shemen Forest)

Why We Omitted It: We visit a monkey sanctuary on day 4, which includes such extras as an open air environment and the ability to feed the animals. If you omit the Yodfat Monkey Park up North, or shorten your excursion there but still want to see monkeys and other animals, this may be a good option.

Where it Goes: Located Halfway between Jerusalem and Tel Aviv, this stop works best on Day 3, either heading towards Tel Aviv or returning. Alternately, you could make it a half day trip from Jerusalem on days 1, 2, 7, 9 or 12

Located at Kfar Daniel, near the Ben Shemen Forest and the city of Modiin, lies a beautiful and vibrant park suitable for family fun and adventure. The landscaping goes for a natural feel, with ponds and waterfalls interspersed between a variety of trees. You'll also find a recreation of an African village, for a feeling like you have instantly been transported to a faraway land.

There are guided tours available, which can last 2-3 hours. They take you by the monkey cages, which house over 250 monkeys of a great variety. You and your children will learn as you go, being exposed to a wealth of wildlife in a fun and relaxed setting. While most of the monkeys are in cages, there is an open air portion in which some monkeys roam free, and you and your children can wander among them.

The wide selection of monkeys includes animals from South America, Asia and Africa. As an added benefit, many of them have been rescued from lab environments or smugglers, and being a part of (by supporting with your admission) the rehabilitative efforts of the park is a meaningful gesture.

There are rest areas and a fast food restaurant on site, as well as a petting zoo for smaller children. This area includes goats, llamas, and other more traditional animals in an up close and personal setting. On weekends, tours are every half hour, however on weekdays they are by appointment only, so **you need to plan ahead**. Additionally, an English guide is not always guaranteed so you will want to inquire before visiting if this is important to you, and make prior arrangements.

TRAVEL TIP: Unlike the Yodfat Monkey park, you cannot picnic here. As an alternative, you can head across the road to nearby Ben Shemen forest where there are great picnic areas.

How to Get Here: From Route # 1, the Tel Aviv- Jerusalem highway take the Ben Shemen interchange and drive toward Kfar Daniel and Gimzo - the park will be on your right and the entrance is clearly signed.

Phone: 08/928- 5888

Email: monkeypk@netvision.net.il

Website: http://ipsf.org.il/?section=51&item=117

Hours: Summer, entrance from 10 AM - 4 PM, stay until 6 PM. Winter, entrance from 10 AM - 3 PM, stay until 5 PM. Fridays all year, entrance from 10 AM - 2 PM, stay until 4 PM.

Approximate Length: 2-3 Hours

Approximate Cost: $12 per person

Jaffa

Why We Omitted It: While a beautiful part of Israel, we chose to schedule the Tel Aviv area for some relaxing beach time. If your family wants to pack in the educational experiences without breaks, this could be great for you.

Where it Goes: Nearest to day 3 in Tel Aviv, can be substituted for that day. Alternately, if you choose to not visit either the North (Days 4-6) or South (Days 10-11) you could plan an excursion around this area instead.

Jaffa (also stylized as Yafo) is a beautiful seaside city in Israel, comprising the southernmost portion of the Tel Aviv-Yafo district. It is also among Israel's oldest cities, with a history dating back thousands of years. Its elevated position overlooking the Mediterranean coast has made it a prime strategic location for the region and trading outpost throughout history.

This "older sister" to Tel Aviv boasts a similarly beautiful coastline, but serves as alternative for those who want to skip the modern city and continue an exploration of antiquity. Here you will skip over the high rises in favor of biblical history (including sites from the stories of Jonah, Solomon, Tabitha, and Saint Peter), along with charming streets, antiquities, churches, galleries, and a glittering fishing port.

The city is filled with old world charm that you can enjoy on a simple aimless stroll, as well as a bevy of landmarks that would allow you to bounce between history and culture on an information packed journey if you so choose. There is so much to see in Jaffa and no wrong way to enjoy it.

If you are interested in a visit, some locations of note are:

- Old Jaffa
- St. Peter's Church
- The IDF History Museum
- Clocktower of Jaffa

- Jaffa Flea Market

- Hagana Museum

- Jaffa Lighthouse

- The Jaffa Museum

Senir (Also known as Snir or Hatsbani) Stream Nature Reserve

Why We Omitted It: Our itinerary includes some great adventures with Israel Extreme. For families looking to take things a little slower, this would be a great substitution.

Where it Goes: North Israel, any of Days 4-6

Representing the Jordan River's longest tributary, the Senir (Hatsbani) Stream is a delight for families, offering great hiking and cool pools for an unforgettable experience. This idyllic nature reserve is a quintessential location for northern Israel, offering a perfect example of the desire to preserve natural beauty and commune with the best features of the land.

It makes for a great family experience, in part because of the variety it offers. Three main trails range from a 10 minute beginner option, to a 30 minute intermediate, and 90 minute advanced trails. Dial in on your family's level of comfort (or decide based on how much energy you have left at that point) and walk comfortably, knowing that whatever trail you choose, you're going to enjoy gorgeous views and get some great exercise.

TRAVEL TIP: The short trail provides a view of a waterfall and follows a wheelchair and stroller accessible route, making it great for families with small children.

In addition to the great natural sights and sounds, you'll find an information center, picnic area, a well-stocked snack-bar, restrooms (great for changing), and a wading pool. You cannot enter the stream itself for swimming, but there are points on the longer trails where you can walk through or across it.

TRAVEL TIP: Waterproof shoes will come in handy here, we recommend Keen water shoes for comfort and reliability.

How to Get Here: Take route 99 east from Kiryat Shemona. The entrance to the reserve is opposite Kibbutz HaGoshrim.

Phone: 04-695-0064

Website:
http://old.parks.org.il/BuildaGate5/general2/data_card.php?Cat=~25~~750558463~Card12~&ru=&SiteName=parks&Clt=&Bur=263561772

Hours: Sunday - Thursday, 8 AM - 5 PM (4 PM in Winter). Friday 8 AM - 3 PM. Closed Saturdays.

Approximate Length: 2 hours

Approximate Cost: $8 per adult, $4 per child for a day pass

Tel Dan National Park

Why We Omitted It: Once again, our itinerary includes some great adventures with Israel Extreme. For families looking to take things a little slower, this would be a great substitution.

Where it Goes: In the Galilee region of Northern Israel, any of Days 4-6

At the heart of this national park is Dan, the ancient and Biblical city that served as the capital of the ancient northern kingdom. You and your family can enjoy the High Place, from the time of King Jeroboam. You'll also find ancient city gates including the newly restored Israelite City Gate and the Canaanite Gate - perhaps the earliest constructed arch ever discovered.

There is a flour mill that operated until 1948 and the ruins of the Canaanite city of Laish, captured by the tribe of Dan during the period of the Judges. Here, history comes alive and combines with hiking for an unforgettable family experience.

The lush setting features the Dan River, one of the major tributaries of the Jordan. Here, water originating from snow melting off Mount Hebron feeds the mighty stream and provides an abundance of plant and animal life to enjoy on your hike. There are three trails of varying difficulty, with the shortest one being wheelchair and stroller accessible.

The circular path takes about 45 minutes and offers an overview of the site at an easy to intermediate difficulty, perfect for most families. Round out your visit with a stop at the restaurant or picnic area to recount your beautiful hike and reflect on the historical and geological wonders of the excavation site.

How to Get Here: Off Highway 99 east of Kiryat Shmona, close to Dag Al Hadan.

Phone: 04-695-1579

Website: http://old.parks.org.il/BuildaGate5/general2/data_card.php?Cat=~25~~970478950~Card12~&ru=&SiteName=parks&Clt=&Bur=437357951

Hours: April - September, 8 AM - 5 PM. October - March, 8 AM - 4 PM.

Approximate Length: 1-2 hours

Approximate Cost: $8 per adult, $4 per child for a day pass

Atlit Detention Camp

Why We Omitted It: Once again, our itinerary includes some great adventures with Israel Extreme. For families looking to take things a little slower, this would be a great substitution.

Where it Goes: In Atlit, just south of Haifa in Northern Israel, any of Days 4-6

During the period of British Mandate for Palestine at the end of the 1930s, Jews were migrating en masse to the land that would become Israel. Many of these immigrants, especially those in Europe, had little choice but to flee for their lives. Unfortunately, the British also felt they had little choice in facing this technically illegal immigration, and so they constructed a detention camp at Atlit. Tens of thousands of Jews were interned here. Declared a national historic site in 1987, the Atlit camp now serves as a museum of the history of Ha'apala.

The camp was again used in the 1940's then housing mostly Holocaust survivors who had fled to the land of Israel for safety. A great escape was planned in 1945, led by them commander Yitzhak Rabin. Palmach special forces broke into the camp and released 200 detainees, all of whom escaped to safety.

On the site now stands a reconstruction of the original camp, complete with barbed wire fence, guard towers, barracks, and areas for classification and disinfection. Among the activities offered are a film about the Palmach break-in, as well as a computerized database containing the names of immigrants, immigration activists and volunteers you can access. This is a fascinating stop for an educational visit, as well as for one interested in researching family history and immigration.

Also on site is a ship, which offers you a chance to experience for yourself the conditions involved in immigration at the time of the camp. See what sort of hardships were endured and feel the pain of those who struggled so hard to reach the cherished land of Israel. This powerful stop will offer an important component of the story of Israel, a nation built by immigrants from all over the world, returning home to the holy land.

PLEASE NOTE: Guided tours of the boat are available in both English and Hebrew, but MUST be booked in advance. Contact them today to inquire.

This detention camp is an important and moving piece of history, though parents should exercise some discretion in deciding if it is too heavy for their children or not. Some of the historical facts, and the imagery of the camp, may be too much for the very young - context should be provided before any visit to such a site.

How to Get Here: From Route 7110 (connects to Route 2), take the exit toward Atlit. Continue on Route 7110 to Amat ha-Mayim Street.

Phone: + 972- (0)4-984-1980

Email: hadracha-atlit@shimur.org.il

Website: http://eng.shimur.org/Atlit/

Hours: Sunday - Thursday, 9 AM - 5 PM. Friday 9 AM - 1PM. **Tours must be booked in advance.**

Approximate Cost: $8 for Adults, $7 for Children

Ein Gedi National Park

Why We Omitted It: Our choices for the Dead Sea region are simply different types of active excursions. Ein Gedi is a beautiful hike and does involve a fair amount of climbing.

Where it Goes: Near Dead Sea, possible substitution on Day 7 or 8

The desert oasis of Ein Gedi, located on the shores of the Dead Sea, has been revered throughout recorded history. Stunning to behold, your family can stand at the lowest place on earth, surrounded by lush nature as you gaze up at the craggy mountains that surround the area.

Here you can enjoy a fantastic hike up, and once there, be able to swim in pools and stand under waterfalls.

The best visits will also take advantage of the history here. Going back more than 5,000 years, this has long been an important place in the history of the Jewish people. King David took refuge in Ein Gedi when he was pursued by King Saul, and rebels fled here from Jerusalem. It served as an important source of balsam for the Greco-Roman era, cementing its importance in the ancient world until its destruction by Byzantine emperor Justinian.

TRAVEL TIP: Nearby you'll find the majesty of Massada, and the Qumran caves, which you could use to expand this site into an entire day near the Dead Sea spent exploring history.

How to Get Here: Located on the western shore of the Dead Sea, just off Route 90

Golani Museum

Why We Omitted It: Originally planned for Day 4, it simply felt like too long a day with too much driving to make sense. If you like the idea better than one of the other Day 4 stops, it makes for a great substitution.

Where it Goes: Ideally day 4, or possibly days 5 or 6, while in Northern Israel

Beginning in 1948 and on through the present day, the Golani Brigade has formed an important part of Israeli history and offers a key insight into the defense of the nation. From the days of a fledgling country struggling to survive, on to the era of international superpower, Israel owes much to its heroes. Brave men and women have fought in, and in some cases given their lives to, the Golani. They deserve honor and respect for their sacrifice.

Also known as the 1st brigade, this most decorated of Israeli Defense Force units has served as an integral part in each of Israel's major conflicts, as well as anti terror efforts and general peacekeeping during the ongoing effort to preserve the safety of the nation. Three of its commanders have gone on to serve as chiefs of staff for the IDF. Besides being a powerful army unit, the Golani Brigade has deep ties to the heritage of Israel, and the indomitable spirit displayed by the sabras and those who helped build the nation from the ground up.

This museum, dedicated to the history and valor of the Golani, will provide context for the rest of your time spent in the north. As you and your family enjoy the fun, excitement and beauty of the region, this stop will help you grow to appreciate those who made your visit possible. That being said, it is not a dour experience in the least. You will enjoy sculptures, items from the soldiers, an audio visual tour, and interactive computerized material. Let the historical brigade come to life through a guided tour (offered in English) and film. Part memorial, part lesson in heroism, this museum has a lot to offer any family.

Address: Located at the junction of routes 65 and 77

Phone: +972-(0)4-6767215

Email Address: golani48@barak.net.il

Website: www.golani.co.il/ (You will need to use a web translator if you do not read Hebrew)

Hours: Sunday - Thursday, 9 AM - 4 PM. Friday, 9 AM - 1 PM. Saturday, 9 AM - 5 PM.

Approximate Time: 1 Hour

Next up is an entire alternate day for Day 8, which sees you rappelling and caving in Central Israel instead of the Dead Sea area:

ALTERNATE Day 8 - Central Israel

Between Jerusalem to the East, Tel Aviv and the Mediterranean coast to the West, lies the central part of Israel that exists outside of the major cities. Here you will find smaller towns, moshavs, and other quaint features in these more suburban environs. Sometimes the place that isn't designated for tourists will teach you the most about a new country, as you see how the people live when the world isn't watching.

The geology of Israel is a fascinating study of its own, with some of the most storied and celebrated stone in the world. With much of the inland nation sitting on top of rich beds of limestone and dolomite, in Israel there is almost as much going on beneath the surface as above.

Jerusalem Stone, *so called for its heavy mining to build the city and its surrounding area, refers to certain types of this stone that have been mined for building since the time of the Bible. Between the harvesting of rock for local structures, export to other areas, and natural erosion and wear due to water and tectonic shifts - Israel sits atop a world of expansive caves, tunnels, grottos, and other unique structures.*

Some of these caves have played a role in history, others have given rise to special plant and animal life. In either case, they provide an interesting study for any family, as well as opportunities for fun and games of an "extreme" nature.

This day, not far outside Jerusalem, in central Israel sees you teaming once more with Israel Extreme. Explore rich cave environments for fun and education with your family. You will literally climb into history on an adventurous day, much of it spent below the surface of the country.

A Beautiful Trip Below The Surface - Tackle Luzit Caves

Stunning Luzit Caves in the Shfela Region are a formation made by ancient excavations and an amazing site to explore together as a family. The soft nature of the limestone here made removing stone and forming such caves easy, with breathtaking results. Israel Extreme knows how to do them right, as you enter deep inside the underground caves and enjoy rappelling through massive hollows down into a large underground hall. Think of it as your family's chance to be a real life Indiana Jones.

Among the stunning network of Luzit Caves are the "bell caves", so called for the interconnected dome-shaped caverns, with a hole in the center at the surface level. They were formed as a result of digging during the Roman, Byzantine, and early Arab periods (3rd - 10th century). While there, take note of the unique shape of the structurally sound domes, as well as the chisel markings on the walls, made by ancient tools and still clearly visible today.

As you wind your way through dark, hidden chambers, you will make your way through to a tunnel, which will spit you out into the surrounding area. This includes natural springs such as Ein Mabua.

According to Israel Extreme, the rappelling is fairly easy and a lot of fun. Luzit Caves are perfect for families because the variety of courses they have to offer ensures everyone in the family, regardless of skill, physicality, or level of experience, can have a great time working at their own pace.

As with other extreme adventures, all activities are optional, no experience is needed and you can opt out at any point if you or a child becomes uncomfortable.

TRAVEL TIP: A headlamp is a useful and inexpensive way to add to your experience here. While you can technically use a flashlight, a headlamp is recommended as you will see more and be free to explore with you hands, or steady yourself in the dark, rocky area. It will also come in handy over the course of your trip as other stops make use of one.

Explore Hidden History - Underground at Bar Kokhba Caves

The Bar Kokhba period was a trying time and important period in history, bittersweet but also inspiring. Simon Bar Kokhba led the third major rebellion by the Jews against Roman oppressors in the years 132-136. The revolt established an independent state over parts of Judea for about three years, and Bar Kokhba was revered as a hero and one who could restore Israel to greatness.

Eventually the rebellion was suppressed with great violence and savagery, as the Talmud describes, particularly at Betar. These events are still at the center of traditional Yom Kippur prayers, and exploring the site where it all took place with your family is a unique and special opportunity to provide context for your lives at home.

These tunnels, used by the rebels during their revolt, are a piece of history and a truly memorable spelunking experience. Walk in the footsteps of Jews who believed in a free and independent state, and who stood for their beliefs against incredible odds.

The caves are tight, and may require some dexterity to get through. Israel Extreme ensures that there are routes for everyone, but this is one activity in which your small children will actually have the easiest time of all. The headlamps will be once again essential, as you'll want your full body available to navigate crevices and search for signs of history left behind. Still, if claustrophobia is a concern for anyone in your family, you may want to reconsider or at least consult before signing on for this activity.

Contact: Interested in this tour? Book through Israel-Extreme (Remember to mention RealFamilyTrips.com for consideration in obtaining a discount)

Website: www.israel-extreme.com

Reference: Sima Sharabi

Office Phone: 04.666.9965

Email: info@israel-extreme.com

Logistics - Alternate Day 8

Suggested Order of Stops:

1. Rappelling in Luzit Caves

2. Explore Bar Kokhba Caves (all can be arranged by Israel Extreme)

Things to Bring/Note:

- Comfortable, athletic clothing and shoes for cave activities

- Headlamps are a necessity to get the most out of the ex-perience

Appendix B: Resources

For those readers looking for even more ideas, great connections, and more detailed background information, we recommend the following resources. Part of our goal in this book has been to provide you with a great vacation, the other part has been about empowering you to make choices and become experts. We want you and your children to arrive in the country already knowing how much fun you are about to have, and we hope that these resources will help allay any flagging concerns, and help you get that much more excited.

These sites represent great tour companies, guides to Israel, and family travel experts who will help further establish you and your children as you plan your trip. Take the time to browse them at your leisure. They may contain other ideas not in these pages that change your plans. They may help confirm that you have made the right choices for your family. They may simply provide more material for you to read in the days leading up to your arrival in Israel, to help raise excitement and get you all prepared for the coming fun.

Some of these resources helped in the writing of this book, others are known to us as valuable sources of information, or reliable providers of services.

RealFamilyTrips.com

www.RealFamilyTrips.com

The website that put this book together, we host a variety of useful information to supplement that in these pages and further help you plan a great trip. Our section of Travel Tips provides articles on a wide variety of topics, many useful for the vacation outlined in this book. From information on converting money, to tips on renewing your passport, taking photos, and reviews of great travel apps - these articles will help you cover both the basics and the extras as you plan a fun a rewarding vacation.

Our Itineraries Section contains days in cities all over the world, much like those you have enjoyed in this book.

FunInJerusalem.com

www.FunInJerusalem.com

Fun In Jerusalem (www.funinjerusalem.com) is a great resource for planning your family vacation to Jerusalem. Their list of recommended activities, family attractions, calendar of events, summer camps guide, and family services will help you plan every detail of your trip. The website is run by Joanna Shebson (joanna@funinjerusalem.com) who loves to inspire family fun.

ATV Tours in Gush Etzion

http://atvtours.co.il/

Just outside of Jerusalem, this company packs knowledgeable guides and high octane excitement into one great package for family fun. Their all terrain vehicle tours span an hour, hour and a half, or two hours - on modern ATV's - and offer a variety of routes. Along the way, guides will stop to show you scenic vistas and provide explanations of what you're seeing, for the perfect blend of excitement and education. This is one tour the kids won't sleep through!

Experienced guides are your gateway to the beauty of Gush Etzion, from major sites and nature reserves, to panoramic views and bumpy "just for fun" trails. They will help you to create an experience that is just right for your family, and cater to your interests as well as the size of your group. To learn more or book a trip, email them: atvgush@gmail.com

The Team at RealFamilyTrips.com

Who Helped Put This Book Together

Our team works tirelessly to bring you the best in travel information and writing, from one real family to countless others. Get to know the group at RealFamilyTrips.com and what makes us different from other family travel resources.

Noah Greenblatt

Noah is 16 years old and just finished his sophomore year in high school. He takes his studies seriously, and loves science. His hobbies include skiing, basketball, baseball, and of course, travel. Noah enjoys hanging out with friends and family. Noah loves time spent vacationing with family and all it has taught him.

Julia Greenblatt

Julia is also a sixteen year old high school student who just completed her sophomore year. She enjoys playing soccer and drawing. In her free time, she volunteers for The Friendship Circle, something she loves to do. Julia's favorite subject is history, and she loves learning about different cultures and civilizations. Julia enjoys the opportunities travelling with family affords her to learn firsthand about the world around her.

Anna Greenblatt

Anna is also a 16 year old who just finished her sophomore year in high school (see a pattern?). She enjoys playing soccer, drawing, reading, and hanging out with her family and friends. Anna is very enthusiastic about helping to make the world a better place through her involvement in charity work, and the chance to see the world through travel helps motivate this passion for service.

Sophia Greenblatt

Sophia just completed 6th grade. She loves ice skating and soccer. Sophia's favorite subject is English. Sophia is excited to share about vacationing with her family and looks forward to time spent with her parents and siblings when they go away together.

Avery Greenblatt

Avery is 9 years old. He just completed 3rd Grade. His favorite hobbies are playing basketball and football. He also loves learning math in school. He enjoys the time that he spends with his family. He is excited to have joined the team at RealFamilyTrips.com and hopes to have a great impact on the site and its goals.

Vera Greenblatt

Vera is a four year old girl (going on 16!) who loves to have fun. She enjoys doing ballet and playing with her siblings. When Vera grows up she wants to be just like her mom! She is the newest member of RealFamilyTrips.com and we look forward to seeing what she can do!

Naomi Greenblatt

Dr. Naomi Greenblatt is an NYU educated psychiatrist who maintains a private practice in reproductive psychiatry. Dr. Greenblatt is a diplomate of the American Board of Psychiatry. She is a frequent lecturer and has been featured on the radio as well as in numerous publications. She is proud to be a co-founder of RealFamilyTrips.com and hopes to help other families achieve the sort of meaningful growth through travel that she has enjoyed with her family.

Jason Greenblatt

Jason Greenblatt Esq is a well known real estate attorney. In addition to his successful career in law, he is an accomplished public speaker and adjunct professor at Yeshiva University. As a co-founder of RealFamilyTrips.com, Jason recognizes travel as an important part of his treasured family time, as well as a powerful tool for growth and education.

Ryan Kagy

Ryan is the Head Writer at RealFamilyTrips.com. Born to a family that valued and celebrated travel, he has known and enjoyed the benefits of a good trip from a young age. He is proud to lead content generation for RealFamilyTrips.com, this volume, and InspireConversation.com. He would like to thank Laura and his parents for their continued love, inspiration, and support in his life.

The "Fine Print"

This book is provided as-is, without any guarantees or warranties of any kind, express or implied. Your use of the book, and the services and vendors mentioned, is at your sole risk. Real Family Trips, Inspire Conversation LLC and each of their members, shareholders, partners, owners and affiliates (all of the foregoing, collectively, the "Publisher and Related Parties") will not be held responsible for any damages of any type due to your use of the book or services and vendors mentioned.

Although Real Family Trips has made every effort to ensure that the information in this book was correct at press time, the author and publisher do not assume and hereby disclaim any liability to anyone for any loss, damage, or disruption caused by errors or omissions, whether such errors or omissions result from negligence, accident, or any other cause.

All information provided in this book is intended for informational and entertainment purposes only. The views expressed are personal opinions only. Neither Real Family Trips nor its parent company Inspire Conversation LLC is responsible for any legal, medical, financial, or other hardships caused by acting on the information provided in this book. Unless otherwise noted, all material in the book is the legal property of Real Family Trips and/or Inspire Conversation LLC and may not be reprinted or republished without the express written consent of Real Family Trips and/or Inspire Conversation LLC. When applicable, every attempt has been made to correctly credit the legal owners of photos and other various media. Please contact us if you feel that you have not been credited properly.

Image Credits

We thank all those who contributed photos and images to help bring Israel to life for this book.

Cover - Original Photo © RealFamilyTrips.com, thanks to Henryez and Derek Aubie for cover formatting and image preparation

Introduction - Ein Gedi Oasis, konstantin32 © 123RF.com

Day 1

- Kotel, Photo © RealFamilyTrips.com
- Old City, Photo © RealFamilyTrips.com

Day 2

- Museum of Underground Prisoners, Photo Courtesy of Museum of Underground Prisoners
- Mahane Yehuda, flik47 © 123RF.com

Day 3

- Tel Aviv Panorama, Zvonimir Atletic © 123RF.com
- Tel Aviv Beach, k45025 © 123RF.com

Day 4

- Monkey, larisap © 123RF.com
- Golan Heights, Asaf Eliason © 123RF.com

Day 5

- Alma Rappelling, Photo Courtesy of Israel Extreme
- Alma Cave Entrance, Photo Courtesy of Israel Extreme

Day 6

- Tornado Boat, Photo Courtesy of Israel Extreme
- Akko, sarkao © 123RF.com

Day 7

- Nachlaot, Borya Galperin © 123RF.com
- Dead Sea, Photo © RealFamilyTrips.com

Day 8

- Shrine of the Book, Borya Galperin © 123RF.com
- Fox's Chimney Salt Crystals, Photo Courtesy of Israel Extreme

Day 9

- Judean Mountains, Kuna George © 123RF.com
- Nitzanim, Rafael Ben-Ari © 123RF.com

Day 10

- Ibexes in Mitzpe Ramon, Sigal Petersen © 123RF.com
- Camel Ride, Photo © RealFamilyTrips.com

Day 11

- Makhtesh Ramon, Robert Hoetink © 123RF.com
- Negev, Photo © RealFamilyTrips.com

Day 12

- Hillside with Olive Trees, Sean Pavone © 123RF.com
- Old Jerusalem City View, Vladislava Marchenko © 123RF.com

Story Part I

- Cave, Galyna Andrushko © 123RF.com

Story Part III

- Kibbutz, Rafael Ben-Ari © 123RF.com

Story Part V

- Painting of Market, andesign101 © 123RF.com

Made in the USA
Columbia, SC
28 November 2019